Feeding your guy

Life and love in the kitchen

Jamie Zettle

Millstone Press

© 2011 Jamie Zettle

Cover and interior design by Todd McGill
Typesetting by Todd McGill
Food styling by Henry Hong and Andrew Culhane
Photography by Lesley M. Austin, lesleyaustinphotography.com
Cover models: Carmela Femia, Rosalia Lamour, Luis Cabrera, Kailani Mag-iba and Ian Zettle

Published by Millstone Press Limited

Published simultaneously in the United States, United Kingdom and Canada

All rights reserved. No part of this publication may be reproduced, stored in a retrieval system, or transmitted in any form or by any means, electronic, mechanical, photocopying, recording or otherwise, without the prior written permission of the publisher. All recommendations are made without guarantee on the part of the author or Millstone Press, Limited. The author and publisher disclaim any liability in connection with the use of the information. For additional information, please contact Millstone Press, 88 George Henry Blvd, Unit 6, North York, Ontario Canada M2J 1E7

First edition: May 2011

Visit the World Wide Web site address for this cookbook at

http://www.feedingyourguy.com

Zettle, Jamie (1968 -)

    Feeding your guy: Life and Love in the Kitchen

    Includes foreword

    ISBN 978-0-9868990-0-3

    1. General cookery. 2. Humour. 3. Commentary. I. Title

Menu

foreword
Food for thought

≈

First dates
Breakfasts, starters, soups, salads

≈

Going steady
Main meals, rice, pasta, vegetables

≈

Happy endings
Sweets, pies, tarts, cookies, squares

I once bought an old copy of the American Woman's Cookbook, published in 1937 for a quarter. It's what would now be considered an old fashioned cookbook, no beautiful pictures, no trendy ingredients, no celebrity chef. Rather, it is a cookbook to feed your family and to create their world. Here's what I mean. There are sections on how to set a table, how to create a guest list, how to prepare food to insure against hardship, how to shop when you are experiencing hardship. In one book, it teaches you how to run your home, support your family, deal with adversity, encourage celebration, nurse your sick, surprise your kids, keep your husband interested in lunch at his desk and make him wonder what will be waiting when he gets home. It teaches you how to love, in a practical, honest way.

When I have a particularly stressful day at work, just before bed, I will curl up on the couch and read that dusty, old 1937 cookbook. I know, clearly cheaper than therapy but perhaps no less necessary. But it takes me somewhere else. It helps me focus on what is important, reminds me to be honest in how I show love. It seems strange but I find it a comfort, this old cookbook whose journey to arrive in my hands is a complete mystery to me. I often wonder who else has flipped through those pages. Who left the smudge of chocolate on the page for brownies? I imagine what smudge I will leave, and who will see it next. It makes me think about what I want my cookbook to be.

The idea for this cookbook grew naturally out of a love of eating. Eating, not cooking, though I enjoy cooking and particularly enjoy shopping for food. Unlike many people, I find the grocery store relaxing and, if I have had a stressful day at work, the place I rush to in order to unwind are the aisles of my local grocery store. I talk a lot about food. I get excited for meal time. I love browsing glossy cookbooks at my local bookstore.

I first brought up the idea of writing a cookbook with my guy appropriately enough at the dinner table. He encouraged me to go for it. The result is this cookbook. My guy and I have been together for four years and married for one. This cookbook is a chronicle of the dishes we enjoyed together while dating, the lessons I learned along the way and the laughter both the food and the insights have provoked. I am convinced that one way to man's heart is through his stomach and I have watched my love for him blossom through the dishes I have prepared. The fact that this cookbook is published is a testament to his patient, encouraging love for me.

No effort of this size is ever done alone. I have been humbled and grateful for the love and support I have received at every step of this journey from my family and many amazing friends. Most of my friends would be embarrassed to see their names in print here, calling out acknowledgment of something which to them is a natural consequence of friendship but, even without naming them each, I cannot let this moment pass without expressing my most profound thanks for their constant support, love, encouragement and occasional cajoling along the way. This cookbook is as much theirs as mine.

I do, however, want to thank my guy. His unfailing support for this project, his encouragement in times of doubt, patience with my outbursts and sacrifices of time and energy reveal clearly the deep blessings of his love for me. I wrote this cookbook for him and with him in my heart. To him, I say thanks. I love you.

It is my sincere wish that you enjoy this cookbook. Laugh, reflect, reminisce, share, disagree, write in the margins and tell your stories. But about all else, eat! Enjoy eating, eat with friends, with family, with your guy. No guilt, no worries, eat! Remember that food was meant to be enjoyable, that it is a pleasure, no apologies. Eat with exuberance!

First dates

I never expected to meet my husband. My life was full. I have a great career, one in which I am still interested. I have a loving family and great friends who fill my life with laughter. I have many interests and an ever-growing list of plans for my future. I never expected that, on an ordinary day, completely unaware, in sloppy clothes and sporting perhaps a pound or two too many, lightning would strike.

I was walking steadily; he was standing, waiting. I was focused on getting somewhere; he was wondering what was next. I saw him standing there; he saw me looking. I looked away; he continued looking. I squared my shoulders and lengthened my stride; he saw me fleeing and turned his shoulders toward me. I caught my breath; he started to smile. I was almost to him; he began to move toward me. My heart began to flutter; he caught my eye. He said hello; I smiled in return.

In that moment, my life began. I never anticipated that, in a fleeting instance, how much I would be changed in meeting my guy. Movement became permanence, though at the time, I was unaware of the change.

I may have met him but I am still me. I love to cook. I was never trained as a chef and I am certainly not a celebrity chef but I do think I am a good cook. I am patient and I am willing to experiment, two characteristics I believe make a great cook. But if you can imagine it, the first time that I cooked a meal for my new guy, I served frozen lasagna and Caesar salad with dressing from a bottle. I was so nervous and so worried that about not making a delicious and memorable meal that I chickened out and served something safe. To his credit and to my opening heart, he ate it happily and complimented me on a delicious dinner.

That first meal taught me a lot about being in a relationship; that fear and worry can paralyze you, that taking it safe always tastes bland, that kindness always soothes the rough spots and that to be a great lover you need to experiment, to be bold. But it also taught me patience. A great dish takes time and so too does a great relationship.

I have cooked countless meals since that first meal in my little apartment with its view of the city skyline, with its mismatched appliances and peeling wallpaper, seated at my little birch-coloured wooden table with its uneven, wobbly chairs. We had many first dates, he and I – evenings of playing pool, snuggled in a movie theatre, late night dinners and early morning phone calls, of flowers arriving at work, and a first pot of soup for a first cold, planning that first vacation away together, worrying over what to pack, checking the mirror three times before leaving the bathroom to head to dinner, always wondering if this guy was the one.

Over the course of those first few months, as I began to know him better and trust him more, I began to cook for him. I personally believe that when you start cooking for your guy, it means something, something significant changes, a history and a future begin at once. It is a gift, a responsibility, an act of courage and fidelity to him. But it is also a gift to you, a gift of discovery, of uncovering, of becoming.

I have many friends who see cooking as a chore, a servitude, a regular, relentless, thankless routine. Even more so, I have friends who have been horrified and repelled by the notion of feeding your guy, that the act demeans you, or diminishes you, or places you second. Occasionally I agree with them, when I am tired or out of sorts but more often I agree with my friends who squeal in excitement with me over a new garlic press or lemon zester.

To me, there is great joy in cooking but more there is great joy in cooking for someone you love. In the early days of our relationship, those first meals were a gift of great joy, given to my guy. He may or may not have been aware that he was even being given a gift but, candidly, in that act, the act of giving a gift freely given, I could first begin sharing my love for him.

When I would run from my apartment building to get into his little car to head off for an evening date or an afternoon of ice skating, I would often be thinking of what I would prepare for dinner at my place or his – new dishes, new tastes.

I watched our relationship blossom in the depths of my mixing bowl, or be rolled out on a floured board as I became more adventurous. I could see my love deepen when I would take a breath of courage and try an untested recipe. I could feel impatience or an unseen hurt show itself as I resented chopping onions or seeding a pomegranate. I would watch myself takes risks, play it safe, experiment, draw back, commit or run away with each choice I made and each dish I choose to prepare.

I watched our relationship grow and flourish and I saw it mirrored in my cooking. Some will laugh and accuse me making cooking spiritual or some sort of sugar-encrusted self-help therapy. To acknowledge those critics is to forget the joy.

These first recipes are like your first dates, new, fresh, a little uncertain, occasionally risky, but always filled with sweet flavours. It is remarkably easy to forget those first nervous days, those stolen kisses, the accidental brush of your hands, the exploration of your tongues, your first shared meals. Every journey, whether in life, in love or at the table, begins with simple gestures. Every beginning should be celebrated – it's the appetizer for all that is to come.

Oatmeal pancakes

We went to my parents yesterday for dinner. I got the opportunity to talk to my Mom about my new adventure in cookbook writing! It wasn't long after we started talking that I was sitting on the floor in front of her old washstand and pulling out her old notebooks and recipe cards filled with all the meals I grew up on. If you can believe, my parents have been married for more than forty years. Imagine if you can the number of meals my mother prepared, feeding her husband and us four kids. Between breakfast, lunch and dinner, over the years, I imagine my mother has prepared over 43 thousand meals!! Talk about feeding your guy! I have to admit she has definitely slowed down in the cooking department and my father picked up the reins. But I certainly realized, sitting leafing through her recipes, we all owe her a huge debt of thanks for all those years of care. I can hardly imagine myself giving half as much or as willingly. I am sure over the next while I will be reflecting more on Mom's gift to us.

½ cup quick cooking oats
½ cup buttermilk
½ cup skim milk
2 egg whites
1 tbsp canola oil
2 tbsp brown sugar, packed
½ tsp salt or to taste
1 tsp baking powder
½ tsp baking soda
½ cup whole wheat flour
½ cup all purpose flour
1 tsp cinnamon

In a medium bowl, combine oats, buttermilk and skim milk. Set aside for 15 to 20 minutes to let the oatmeal soften.

Beat in the egg whites and oil and mix well. Add sugar, salt and cinnamon, then the baking powder, baking soda and flour. Stir just until moistened.

Heat a lightly oiled or non-stick griddle over medium heat. For each pancake pour about 1/8 cup of batter onto the griddle. Turn when the tops are covered with bubbles and the edges look cooked. Turn only once.

Fluffy white pancakes

I was given this recipe by my guy's sister, my future sister-in-law. How much can we learn about our families by the recipes they cherish, their generosity in sharing and the joy they find in giving. I make these pancakes now for my guy, thinking of my new sister. This recipe exchange was one of the first moments of connection between my sister-in-law and I and I still have the flower-covered recipe card with her looping handwriting upon it. It was a loving act, this recipe, from her to me; it meant inclusion and acceptance, it meant a reaching out of hands, the pancakes taste of love.

2 cups flour
5 tsp baking powder
3 tbsp white sugar
2 tsp salt
2 eggs, beaten
2 cups milk or 1 ½ cups for fluffier cakes
4 tbsp canola oil

Mix dry ingredients and combine with wet. Do not over mix. Spoon onto hot griddle. Cook until bubbling, flip and finish cooking.

Breakfast oatmeal

I was given this recipe by our dear friend, Carmela. She has taught me how to make authentic tomato sauce, always up for a laugh and is a great friend to us. When she started taking hot yoga, her nutritionist recommended this healthy breakfast, some complex carbohydrates and protein, a great way to start your day. The best part – it taste great.

1 ½ cups quick cooking oatmeal
3 cups water
1 tbsp peanut butter
1 ripe banana, mashed

Combine the ingredients in a saucepan and cook on medium heat until oatmeal thickens and peanut butter is melted. Also, delicious if you substitute the peanut butter and banana with a dash of cinnamon and a handful of raisins. For creamier oatmeal, mix ingredients together and put in the fridge overnight and heat as instructed the next morning.

Cheese and tarragon pancakes with fruit salsa

I made these pancakes on the first morning after we moved in together. Carrying plates of these savoury pancakes to our little table and sitting down opposite my guy in what would become my place, I realized that unusual combinations often have surprisingly, delicious results.

1 cup whole wheat flour
1 tbsp baking powder
2 tsp sugar
1 cup milk
2 eggs
½ tsp vanilla
¼ to ½ tsp ground cinnamon
1 tbsp fresh tarragon, chopped or
1 tsp dried tarragon
1 ½ cups Gouda, grated
Butter or canola oil for cooking

Apple and Pineapple salsa

½ cup apple, diced
½ cup pineapple, diced
1 tbsp lemon juice
3 tbsp maple syrup
1 tsp fresh tarragon, chopped

In a small bowl, mix salsa ingredients. Leave at room temperature while making pancakes.

In a large bowl, combine flour, baking powder, sugar and cinnamon. Make a hole in the middle and pour in milk. Stir with a whisk to obtain a smooth batter.

Add eggs, vanilla and tarragon. Mix well and add cheese. Heat a skillet over medium heat, melt in butter and pour a small ladleful of batter. Cook for four minutes or until bubbles appear in pancake and first side is golden. Turn pancake over, continue cooking for three minutes. Batter should be fully cooked in the centre. Repeat steps until all the batter is used.

Serve pancakes warm and topped with apple and pineapple salsa.

Ham and cheese flan

When I was a child, I used to love to wake up to or walk in the door for lunch and smell this flan baking in the oven, its rich flavours escaping, setting my mouth to water. We would often eat it served with a garden salad. I loved the flaking tenderness of the crust, the sharp bite of the cheese, the delicious musky flavour of the mushrooms. This flan always reminds me that simplicity prevails – and straightforward is often the best path in love.

1 – 9 inch unbaked pie shell
2 tbsp butter
½ cup chopped onion
½ cup chopped mushrooms
1 cup cubed ham
1 ½ cup shredded old cheddar cheese
2 eggs, beaten
1 ¼ cup milk
¼ cup flour
½ tsp salt, pepper

Preheat oven to 375F degrees. Sauté onion and mushrooms in butter. Sprinkle ham, cheese, onions and mushrooms in pie shell. Combine eggs and milk; gradually blend in flour, salt and pepper. Pour into pie shell.

Bake 30 to 40 minutes at 375F degrees. Let stand for five minutes before cutting.

Asparagus and red pepper quiche

You may find yourself thinking of Christmas colours when you make this dish but it is good anytime of the year. Tender young asparagus and sweet red peppers give this quiche a slightly sweet and delicate taste. Serve with soup or salad for a nice spring dinner.

1 deep 9 inch pastry shell
1 tbsp Dijon mustard
1 tbsp vegetable oil
1 small onion, chopped
1 lb fresh asparagus, trimmed, coarsely chopped
½ sweet red pepper, cut in thin strips
3 tbsp finely chopped fresh dill
1 ½ cups grated Swiss cheese
3 eggs
1 cup milk
salt and pepper to taste

Preheat oven to 375F degrees.

Spread mustard evenly over pastry. Sauté onion, asparagus and red pepper in oil until tender crisp. Remove from heat. Stir in cheese and dill. Spread evenly in pastry shell.

Beat eggs, milk, salt and pepper. Pour over vegetables mixture. Bake in oven for 35 to 45 minutes or just until set and golden brown. Cool 10 minutes before slicing.

Bacon and cheese quiche

What can I say? This is my easy version of Quiche Lorraine minus the sun drenched fields of lavender, the oaken barrels of wine, the cheese mongers and tall, handsome, accent-laden Frenchmen. Fortunately it tastes as good and saves you an airfare.

6 slices of bacon, diced
2 tbsp flour
3 eggs
1 cup milk
1 cup tomato sauce
¼ tsp basil
¼ tsp oregano
1 9 inch unbaked pie shell
2/3 cup grated mozzarella cheese
1 tbsp onion, minced

Preheat oven to 400F degrees.

Cook bacon until crisp; set aside. Blend flour with eggs; beat in milk, tomato sauce, basil and oregano. Set aside.

Bake pie shell for 5 minutes. Remove, cover bottom of crust with 1/3 cup cheese, sprinkle on onion, bacon and then remaining cheese. Pour egg mixture carefully over all.

Bake at 400F degrees for 15 minutes. Reduce heat to 325F degrees and bake for 25 to 30 minutes longer until firm.

Breakfast trout – A fisherman's delight

I learned a little of difference. My guy, so similar to me, is in many ways often a complete alien. His thoughts, tastes, directions and approaches often stand in stark contrast to my own. In dating, I let myself celebrate his differences, the times when I did not understand him, the paths I could not walk, the choices I would not make. I learned to let go, understand that control is pointless, that freedom brings new life. When I had just begun to know him, I suddenly wanted to change him – and then I freed him again to be different than me. Trout for breakfast is different – be free, try it.

10 fillets of trout
1 tsp salt
2 eggs, beaten
dash of Tabasco or hot sauce
1 cup cornflake crumbs
½ cup oil

In a skillet heat the oil. Prepare fillets by washing, pat dry and halve. Dip fillets into a bowl of beaten egg, hot sauce and salt. Toss in a bowl of crumbs, coating each side thoroughly. Fry until golden brown turning only once. Serve with sliced tomatoes, toast and coffee.

Wife saver breakfast casserole

I made this casserole for breakfast on our first Christmas morning. I would much rather be nestled amid piles of torn paper, sitting sideways on an errant bow, dodging the camera in my Santa pyjamas, sipping juice beside him, reflecting the glow of lights from the tree – than sweating in the kitchen. Just this once!

12 slices bread, crusts removed
1 tbsp olive oil
8-10 large slices back bacon or rashers
1 cup mushrooms, cleaned, sliced thinly
2 medium onions, chopped
½ cup baby spinach, washed
1 large tomato, sliced thinly
1 tsp dried basil
2 cups old cheddar cheese, shredded
10 eggs, beaten
½ cups milk
2 cups cornflakes, crushed or breadcrumbs

In a lightly greased glass-baking dish, place bread slices in an even layer over the bottom of the baking dish. Set aside.

In a large skillet, heat the oil and fry bacon in batches. Remove from pan when cooked and drain on absorbent paper. In remaining oil, add mushroom and onion, cook, stirring occasionally, until tender, about 7 minutes. Remove from pan from heat.

Arrange bacon slices atop bread, sprinkle evenly with mushroom and onions. Add spinach, covering pan evenly and top with tomato slices. Sprinkle with dried basil and cover pan evenly with shredded cheese. Top with second layer of bread slices.

In a medium bowl, whisk together eggs and milk and pour over baking dish, soaking through bread slices. Cover baking dish and refrigerate overnight.

Preheat oven to 350F degrees. Remove baking dish from fridge, unwrap and cover with crushed cornflakes or breadcrumbs. Bake in oven for 1 hour or until set. Allow to stand 10 minutes before cutting.

Homemade granola

Perfect for feeding him when everyone is in a rush. Easy to make, store and serve, this granola makes an easy breakfast when you want to oversleep or a delicious snack to simply dump into your palm and toss in your mouth.

2 ½ cups rolled oats
½ cup sliced almonds
½ cup broken walnuts
½ cup chopped pecans
½ cup sesame seeds
½ cup wheat germ
½ cup shredded coconut
½ cup sunflower seeds, unsalted and shelled
½ cup safflower oil
½ cup honey
½ cup dried cranberries
½ cup raisins
½ cup currants

Preheat oven to 325F degrees. In a very large bowl, place oats, almonds, walnuts, pecans, sesame seeds, wheat germ, coconut and sunflower seeds. Mix together with your hands to combine well. In a small saucepan, combine oil and honey over medium heat and warm through, stirring. Pour over ingredients in bowl and mix well.

Spread mixture sparsely on a number of sided baking sheets and bake for 15 minutes. Stir mixture and bake a further 15 minutes until golden brown. Remove and allow to cool. Pour into a large mixing bowl and stir in cranberries, raisins and currants. Store in an airtight container.

Blueberry French toast bake

This recipe is initially a bit of work. You will find yourself trimming crusts from bread, washing berries, spreading cheese, mixing cream and wondering is it worth it. Try this, prepare this dish the night before, get up early and drive o a cottage on a lake and pop it in the oven. When it is ready, take your guy outdoors on the deck, drizzle with real maple syrup, serve with more fruit and hot coffee and together watch the mist burn off the lake.

1 ½ cups blueberries
12 oz spreadable cream cheese
18 slices bread, thick sliced
10 eggs
¼ cup pure maple syrup
½ cup melted butter
2 ½ cups half and half cream

Spray a 13 by 9 inch baking dish and set aside. In a small mixing bowl, gently fold half the blueberries into the cream cheese. Spread this mixture onto 9 of the bread slices. Top with remaining slices of bread. Trim off crusts and cut "sandwiches" into 1 inch cubes. Place cubes in prepared baking dish. Sprinkle remaining blueberries over bread cubes.

In a medium-mixing bowl, whisk together eggs, maple syrup, butter and cream. Pour mixture over bread cubes. Cove with plastic wrap and press down so cubes are covered in cream-egg mixture. Refrigerate overnight.

Preheat oven to 350F degrees. Bake for 40 minutes or until top is golden brown and centre is set. Serve warm with additional maple syrup and orange zest.

Welsh toast

Have the girls over for a sleepover, like you did as a child. Buy new pyjamas, sit up late, talk, laugh, cry, watch old black and white romance movies and enjoy being together. For breakfast, serve these toasts with fresh juice and fruit and decide who is hosting next.

1 loaf egg bread, sliced 1 inch thick, approx. 9 slices
4 eggs, plus 2 egg whites
½ cup sugar
3 cups milk
1 tbsp Grand Marnier
grated zest of 1 orange
1 tsp nutmeg

Arrange bread slices on a large baking sheet. In a large mixing bowl, whisk together eggs, egg whites, sugar, liqueur and orange zest. Pour this mixture over bread slicing, ensuring each slice is saturated with liquid. Cover and let stand 1 hour or overnight.

Preheat oven to 400F degrees. On a lightly oiled griddle, brown both sides of bread slices, removing them to a non-stick baking sheet as you work. When all slices are browned, bake for 20 minutes in oven. Serve hot with maple syrup and a dusting of icing sugar.

Decadent eggs Benedict with asparagus

We had been dating only a short while when I met some dear friends of my guy who have since become great friends to me as well. From Quebec City, they are voracious about life, grabbing each day with passion, savouring each taste, sound, moment. Every aspect of life is a cause for laughter and shared joy. They remind me to appreciate my guy and to regularly remember that decadence and indulgence ought to play a looming role in the most ordinary of days.

3 English muffins, halved and toasted
6 eggs
1 tbsp vinegar
1 tbsp oil
6 slices back bacon, cooked
24 spears asparagus, blanched
18 slices Brie, ½ inch thick
Hollandaise sauce to garnish

Lightly toast English muffins. Set aside. In a small skillet, heat oil and cook bacon till cooked but not crisp. Remove from pan and drain on absorbent paper. In a small pot, bring salted water to a boil and quickly blanch asparagus. Remove from water and refresh under cold water and set aside. In a small saucepan, prepare Hollandaise sauce and keep warm.

To prepare, place toasted muffins on plate, and first layer bacon, then asparagus, then Brie on the muffin. Fill a shallow skillet with water and add vinegar. When water is just bubbling but not boiling, drop eggs into the water and poach for 2 ½ - 3 minutes. Remove eggs from water with slotted spoon. Place hot egg on Brie and cover with Hollandaise sauce. Serve surrounded by fresh fruit. Serve hot and immediately.

Cream cheese ball

For my birthday one year, my guy arranged a surprise party for me with all my closest friends and family. Walking into a room filled with floating balloons and laughter from friends was a joyous moment. My guy had made a huge buffet table of food, all displayed lovingly. This recipe is his and is amazing on cream crackers.

1 package of cream cheese
¼ cup dry cranberries
1/8 tsp cinnamon
2 tbsp orange juice
1 tbsp orange rind
1 tbsp white sugar

Combine all ingredients in a large mixing bowl, ensuring the cream cheese is well mixed with other ingredients. Form into a ball and place on wax paper. Wrap the paper around the ball to maintain its shape and refrigerate until needed.

Classic crab cakes

We live in an age of prepared, frozen hors d'oeuvres sold in cardboard boxes in the freezer section of the grocery store, their branding promising entertainment and good times. Inevitably, they taste bland and rubbery. These cakes, with a hint of tang and a bit of a kick, are sure to impress.

1 large egg, lightly beaten
2 tbsp mayonnaise
1 tsp Dijon mustard
1 tsp Worcestershire sauce
1 tbsp Tabasco sauce
½ red onion, minced
1 celery stalk, minced
½ red pepper, minced
1 tbsp chives, finely chopped
½ cup breadcrumbs
1 lb cook crabmeat, pulled apart
salt and pepper to taste
2 tbsp butter
2 tbsp olive oil

In a large bowl, combine egg, mayonnaise, mustard, Worcestershire sauce, Tabasco, onion, celery, red pepper and chives. Mix well and then add breadcrumbs, crabmeat salt and pepper. Using a fork, blend ingredients well. Divide mixture into 8 portions and shape into patties and ¾ inch thick.

In a large skillet, warm half the butter and oil over medium-high heat. Fry half the crab cakes for about 4 minutes on each side until golden brown, turning once. Repeat with remaining cakes, butter and oil. Serve immediately.

Caramelized onion and mushroom dip

Everyone serves hummus. A few adventurous friends serve baba ganoush. The truly exotic serve roasted red pepper dip. Be original and prepare this smoky, richly sweet dip and serve it with toasted Melba rounds. For a richer flavour, add 1 tbsp of port or Madeira and leave those hummus-making friends in awe.

2 tsp canola oil
2 onions, chopped
3 cups mushrooms, quartered
2 cloves garlic, minced
¼ cup fresh parsley, chopped
½ tsp salt
¼ tsp pepper
1 ¼ cup light sour cream
1/3 cup light mayonnaise
¼ cup chopped fresh chives

In a non-stick skillet, heat oil over medium heat; add onions and cook, stirring occasionally, until softened, about 10 minutes. Reduce heat to medium low and cook, stirring often, until evenly golden, about 30 minutes.

Meanwhile, in a food processor or using knife, finely chop mushrooms. Add to pan along with garlic, parsley, salt and pepper. Increase heat to medium high; sauté until no liquid remains, 8 to 10 minutes. Scrape into bowl; allow to cool.

Stir in sour cream, mayonnaise and half of the chives. Transfer to serving bowl. To serve, sprinkle with remaining chives. You can make this recipe ahead, simply cover and refrigerate for up to 3 days.

Apple and red onion marmalade

I believe that it is in the smallest gestures, the unseen deeds, the time taken, that we display the true depth of our love for our guy. Love can come in little flourishes, in those small additions that transform the ordinary into the extraordinary. This apple and onion marmalade is surprisingly sophisticated when made and adds a touch of class when served with steak, chicken or as a garnish on a grilled burger.

2 tbsp butter
2 tbsp olive oil
8 cups sliced red onions
3 tbsp sugar
¼ tsp salt
½ tsp ground cloves
½ tsp cinnamon
½ cup red wine
½ cup red wine vinegar
½ cup apple cider
2 tbsp honey
4 cups apples, cored, peeled and sliced

In a large saucepan, melt the butter in the oil over low heat. Add the onions and stir to coat with mixture. Cover loosely and cook for 10 minutes, stirring occasionally. Add sugar, salt, cloves, cinnamon, wine, vinegar, cider and honey. Stir well and continue cooking uncovered until onions are soft, about 20 minutes. Add the apples and cook for a further 15 minutes until apples soften and whole mixture becomes thick and jam-like. Remove from heat and cool. Pack into hot, sterilized glass jars and store in refrigerator for one month.

Garlic spread

I first tired garlic spread at family Sunday barbeques while staying with friends in Australia. Lebanese by descent, garlic was and remains an important part of their cuisine, even as they have adapted and adopted many aspects of traditional Australian cuisine. They prepare this spread by pounding raw garlic, oil and salt and making a thick paste. It is delicious with sizzling barbequed chicken or hot grilled potato slices. This version is much milder but equally delicious.

2 heads garlic, separated into cloves, skins on
1 cup vegetable broth
2 cups water
½ tbsp olive oil

In a small saucepan, combine the garlic, broth and water; bring to a boil over high heat. Reduce heat and simmer, uncovered, for about an hour or until almost all the water has been evaporated.

Run the garlic and remaining liquid through a food mill. Discard skins. Place the garlic mash in a bowl and mix well with oil. Season with salt to taste. Serve on toasted slices of bread.

Spicy cornbread

I first learned how to make Johnny cake or cornbread at Friendly Acres. I would mix the cornmeal and buttermilk in a big crockery bowl and pour the batter into long, deep aluminum pans. Baked, I would slice it and place the squares hot into baskets to be served with chilies or soups or just eaten hot smothered in butter. I love spicy food so I have modified the original recipe to give this dish slightly more punch.

2 cups cornmeal
4 cups flour
2 tsp baking powder
1 tsp baking soda
2 tsp salt
2 eggs beaten
2 cups buttermilk
2 tbsp olive oil
5 chipotle or jalapeno peppers, chopped finely
1 bunch chives, chopped finely

Preheat oven to 350F degrees. Blend all wet ingredients together then add the dry ingredients and mix well. Transfer the mixture to a well-greased loaf pan and bake in oven for 45 minutes.

Dijon deviled eggs

I learned yesterday that the average child would eat over 1500 peanut butter and jam sandwiches before they graduate from high school! Now admittedly, this is probably a uniquely North American behaviour and taste but one that was certainly true for me! How many of us can remember those peanut butter and jam sandwiches, taken from your lunch bag and eaten at your desk in grade school, seated on hard green formed seats, that green metal tube traversing from your seat to the table, the top of your desk scratched and etched by fellow class mates of years past. Open the now wrinkled wax paper and taking out your sandwich, the white bread slightly squished, the peanut butter warm, the jam escaping from the sides, the taste delicious! Even now nothing speaks of comfort food more to me than a PB sandwich or toast with peanut butter and jam. Despite tasting foods from around the world and filling my cupboards with goodies both exotic and local, I still reach for peanut butter and homemade jam, made by my mother's hand and now even by mine, slathered on bread and enjoyed with a cold glass of milk. A timeless classic! Here is another timeless classic.

6 hard-boiled eggs
2 tbsp mayonnaise
1 ½ tsp Dijon mustard
1 green onion, very thinly sliced
Freshly ground black pepper
Salt to taste
Paprika, optional

Halve or quarter eggs; scoop yolks into a small bowl. Mash well; add mayonnaise and Dijon until desired consistency is reached. Stir in white part of sliced onion and most of the chopped parsley. Taste and add salt and pepper to taste. Using a small teaspoon or pastry bag, fill egg white halves or quarters. Sprinkle with sliced green onion and remaining parsley. Sprinkle with a little pepper and/or paprika, if desired.

Guacamole

My guy taught me how to make guacamole, how to remove the pit from the avocado without disturbing the meat, the importance of the freshest ingredients and the rewards of patience. Allow yourself to learn; allow him to teach. It is both pairs of hands that build your life.

3 avocados, halved, seeded, and peeled
1 lime, juiced
½ tsp salt
½ tsp cumin
½ tsp cayenne
½ medium onion, diced
2 Roma tomatoes, seeded and diced
1 tbsp chopped cilantro
1 clove garlic, minced

In a large bowl place the scooped avocado pulp and lime juice, toss to coat. Drain, and reserve the lime juice, after all of the avocados have been coated. Using a potato masher add the salt, cumin, and cayenne and mash. Then, fold in the onions, tomatoes, cilantro, and garlic. Add 1 tablespoon of the reserved lime juice. Let sit at room temperature for one hour then serve.

Seven layer taco dip

My sister-in-law served this dish the first occasion my guy and I visited my brother's place. With great enthusiasm did my guy enjoy this dip, commenting that it was a memory of his and an almost forgotten treat. Dating reveals surprising connections – and gives you the chances to connect over a tortilla chip!

1 package taco seasoning mix
1 16 oz can refried beans
1 8 oz package cream cheese, softened
1 16 oz sour cream
1 16 oz jar of medium salsa
1 large tomato, chopped
1 green bell pepper, diced finely
1 bunch green onions, chopped
2 cups sharp Cheddar cheese, shredded

In a medium bowl, blend the taco seasoning mix and refried beans. Spread the mixture onto a large serving platter.

Mix the sour cream and cream cheese in a medium bowl. Spread over the refried beans.

Top with salsa. Place a layer of tomato, green bell pepper and green onions over the salsa and cover all with Cheddar cheese and serve.

Artichoke puffs

An old girlfriend of mine at university gave me this recipe. I remember the glasses of cold, white wine, the endless chats, the laughter, and standing in her kitchen, a glass in one hand, the other waving to make some point and she there, stooped over, oven door open, the white stovetop framing her blond hair as she looked back at me to hear to me, red and white oven mitts dwarfing her tiny hands and her pulling a hot baking sheet from beneath the broiler, the topping sizzling golden brown, the black spatula passing me one, the hot melba toasting my fingertips, the taste stopping conversation.

1 ½ cups grated old cheddar cheese
1 ¾ cups + 2 tbsp mayonnaise
½ tsp onion salt
¼ tsp lemon pepper
14 oz can marinated artichoke hearts
Melba toast rounds

Mix cheese, mayonnaise, onion salt and lemon pepper well and refrigerate until serving time.

Cut artichoke hearts into 4 or 5 pieces and set aside until serving time.

At serving time, place Melba rounds on a baking sheet. Top with a piece of artichoke and cover with approximately 1 heaping tsp of cheese mixture.

Broil until cheese melts and bubbles and starts to turn light brown. Be careful not to burn. Serve immediately.

Lip smacking shrimp

Shrimp on the Barbie! I lived for eight months in Sydney, Australia, staying with friends. I was between jobs and took my savings, bought a ticket and landed looking for an adventure and chance to reconnect with myself. It was a wild time, tasting wines in the Hunter valley, eating Greek food late into the night at cafes in Melbourne, feeding kangaroos, snorkeling on the Great Barrier Reef and falling off my surfboard during lessons at Bondi Beach. This shrimp recipe tastes just right when grilled to perfection, eaten immediately and washed down with a cold beer.

½ lb shrimp, deveined and de-shelled

Marinade:

Juice of two limes
4 tbsp chopped coriander
1 tbsp olive oil
1 tbsp sugar
2 cloves garlic minced
1 tbsp curry powder or curry spice mix
½ tsp ground cumin
¼ tsp ground coriander
salt and pepper to taste

Mix marinade ingredients, add shrimp and marinate at room temperature for a minimum of 30 minutes. Stir-fry or grill shrimp on skewers. You can also keep sauce with the shrimp after stir-frying, add some vegetables, cook and serve over rice or noodles.

I got out of bed this morning and walked straight into the kitchen and reached into my lazy Susan and pulled out my favourite crockery bowl. I know I am even smiling at myself as I write this and shaking my head, seriously there may be something wrong with me. Quite soon I am almost certain, little men, not in stark white coats smelling slightly of bleach and hand sanitizer and offering snug fitting coats that clasp at the back but rather in my case little men in stark white aprons smelling slightly of flour and nutmeg and offering the newest in Teflon coated, raised baking sheets will come suddenly through my front door and escort me out and into a sparkling clean doughnut truck to take me somewhere quiet for a rest! Anyway doesn't everyone get out of bed and walk immediately into their kitchen and pull out their favourite bowl and feel comforted and pleased?

I pulled out my bowl and just held it and look at it all around. I suppose I must have been dreaming about it or thinking about it as I awoke. It was my grandmother's bowl. It is a thick crockery bowl, medium to large sized, cream-coloured with two thick blue bands around its lip. The finish has been muted, almost buffed natural, by the endless washing that poor bowl has endured over its life. It has a soft texture, the inside scored gently by spoons pushing around its sides. I am not sure where Grandma ever got the bowl, whether it was a gift for Christmas or she bought it at Sears or whether it was a found, for a nickel, on a church bazaar table nestled besides hand knitted mittens and tea cozies.

But I remember that bowl throughout my childhood. Coming in off the hills outside her house, cold from riding our sleigh, it would be on the counter, Grandma making us tea biscuits and hot chocolate when we came in from the cold, hot biscuits covered in butter and honey emerging from that bowl, and served to us at the table to warm up. I know she would have made pies and desserts, dinners and lunches in that bowl for my own mother when she was a child, Mom's favourites emerging from that bowl. Grandma's hands would have washed it, standing at her sink looking out the window at the garden and the bush beyond. My hands travel where hers once did as I clean it after feeding my guy. My mother gave me the bowl when Grandma passed away. I had just left for university and I am sure my mother, ever practical, gifted me the bowl knowing that I would be setting up my apartment, having nothing, needed everything. But Mom gave me much more. I have a piece of my history, my mother's and my grandmother's history. I have a deep affection for that bowl, almost for the bowl itself. I love each chip out of the crockery and the marks inside, the way the blue is fading. I will almost always choose that bowl over any other even when it is the wrong bowl to choose by size or by design. Some dishes you simply need a wooden bowl for in order to get the right roughness for blending ingredients, but even then, I will often choose my favourite and have less than perfect results.

Does it seem strange to be rising from a flu and the first thing I did this morning is walk to the kitchen and get out my bowl? And now frankly I have talked about it for paragraphs! Yes, something is deeply off centre in me! Perhaps I just find the bowl comforting. And in this world, I take comfort from what I can. It makes me happy. Hope you have a similar bowl.

Couscous and chickpea patties

These patties make equally good hors d'oeuvres or stand as a quick, nutritious, flavour filled lunch. Even cold, they make a delicious sandwich and a wholesome alternative to lunch meat.

1 cup vegetable stock
½ cup couscous
1 tsp dried basil
1 can chick peas, drained
Rind of one lemon
1 egg
2 tbsp water
1 clove garlic, minced
¼ tsp each salt and pepper
1 tsp canola oil
2 whole wheat pita breads
½ cup light sour cream
2 cups shredded lettuce
½ cup sliced cucumber
¼ cup sliced radishes

In a saucepan, bring stock to boil. Remove from heat, stir in couscous, basil and lemon rind. Cover and let stand for 5 minutes. Fluff with fork.

In a food processor, chop chick peas finely. Add couscous mixture, onions, egg, water, garlic, salt and pepper, mix until combined. Shape into four ½ inch thick patties.

In a non-stick skillet, heat oil over medium high heat, cook patties, turning once, for 8 minutes until golden.

Cut pita bread in half. Open to form pocket. Spread with sour cream. Fill with patty, lettuce, cucumber and radishes.

Old fashioned lobster pot

A friend of mine from Nova Scotia gave me this recipe, a little down East flavour from a place known as much for its rugged coastline, foggy mornings and salt-sprayed, colourful houses as for the sheer warmth of its people. At one time, lobster was considered poor man's food and kids were embarrassed to take it as sandwiches for lunch in tin boxes. Today, it has been redeemed and this pot is a great way to enjoy it.

2 cups cooked lobster meat
1 loaf round, unsliced pumpernickel bread
8 oz package of light cream cheese
1 cup light sour cream
1 tsp Worcestershire sauce
½ tsp Tabasco sauce
1 ½ tsp garlic, minced
2 cups grated cheddar cheese
½ cup green onion, chopped
dash of salt and pepper

Preheat oven to 350F degrees.

Drain lobster, cut into bite size pieces. Hold in refrigerator.

Slice top off of bread. Scoop out inside of bread, leaving a 1 inch layer around outside and bottom. Reserve bread, cut into cubes for dipping.

In a large bowl, cream the cream cheese. Add sour cream, Worcestershire, Tabasco and garlic; mix well. Fold in grated cheddar cheese, green onions, salt and pepper. Fold in lobster.

Fill bread shell with lobster mixture. Place top on bread loaf; wrap in foil. Place on baking sheet and bake for 70 minutes until mixture is thoroughly heated.

Serve with bread cubes, crackers or cut up fresh vegetables.

Smoked salmon mousse

This spread is remarkably simple to prepare but shows very well at dinner parties or on buffet tables. I learned how to prepare this delicacy from a member of the trout club. I spent part of one afternoon, usually once a week, smoking trout that members had caught over apple wood after rinsing the fish of homemade brine. One member nudged his way in and smoked his salmon amid my trout. Later, he quickly showed me how to prepare this elegant spread with few ingredients but all of them of the highest and freshest quality. Later at dinner in the dining room, his wife was suspicious of our clandestine looks and shared laughs; little would she guess I was exchanging recipes with an old fisherman.

½ lbs finely minced smoked salmon
2 tbsp butter
4 tbsp double cream
1 tbsp olive oil
pinch of cayenne
2 tbsp lemon juice

Cream the butter and oil together, add finely minced salmon and blend thoroughly. Beat in lemon juice, cayenne and cream. Fill ramekins and smooth tops and chill, serve with hot toast.

Argentinean Chimichurri sauce

I have never been to Argentina but imagine it to be a land of startling natural beauty, raging rivers, endless skies, fields of cattle, warm people. This blended sauce served over steak or fish adds bite to the dish and compliments the meat well. I imagine Argentina will appear on a wish list for my guy and I in the future for a vacation and I hope to find myself sampling this same sauce made with care by an Argentinean chef. I hope to pick up a few pointers.

1 cup lightly packed chopped flat leaf parsley
3-5 cloves garlic, minced
1 tsp salt
½ tsp freshly ground black pepper
½ tsp chili pepper flakes
2 tbsp fresh oregano leaves
2 tbsp shallot or onion, minced
¾ cup olive oil
3 tbsp sherry wine vinegar or red wine vinegar
3 tbsp lemon juice

Place all ingredients in a blender or food processor and pulse until well chopped but not puréed. Spoon over steak, grilled fish or chicken.

Mushroom risotto cakes

I had these succulent treats first at a party on Christmas Eve and could not resist perching beside the plate and eating one after the next. I only barely resisted filling my pockets with them when leaving. Once home, I experimented with these cakes; the result is this recipe. My guy loves mushrooms and these cakes have become another way to satisfy his desire. They smell wonderful while cooking and are a great hors d'oeuvre for any party.

4 tbsp butter or olive oil
Sea salt
Freshly ground white pepper
1 large onion, chopped
2 cloves garlic, minced
½ cup mushrooms, peeled, stalks removed, thinly sliced
1 bay leaf
1 ½ cup Arborio rice
3 cups water or vegetable stock
1 cup freshly grated Parmesan cheese
1 tbsp fresh thyme leaves
1 cup flour
2 eggs, lightly beaten
1 cup breadcrumbs
Vegetable or olive oil

Melt butter in a heavy saucepan, season and cook gently onion and garlic until soft about 10 minutes. Add mushrooms and bay leaf and cook for 10 minutes or until soft. Add rice and 2 ½ cups of water or stock. Simmer and stir until rice is cooked, adding more water or stock as needed. Discard bay leaf and stir in Parmesan and thyme. Transfer to a bowl and allow to set in the fridge. Shape into 4 to 6 round cakes with your hands. Lightly dust in flour, dip in egg and then coat evenly with breadcrumbs. Shallow or deep-fry in oil until golden brown and warm in centre about 6 minutes. Serve with green salad.

Moroccan eggplant

I love eggplant; my guy hates it. This preparation is our compromise, eggplants flavoured with the tastes of dusky, spice souks, sultry heat, slow cooking and meals shared among family. This dish makes a terrific meze or starter for a celebratory meal, especially nice when paired with a cooling Moroccan carrot soup.

2 eggplants
1 tbsp salt
2 red peppers
1 tsp cumin seeds
3 tbsp olive oil
2 cloves garlic, minced
1 tsp salt
½ tsp red pepper flakes
1 cup tomato sauce or chopped diced tomatoes
Juice of one lemon
3 tbsp chopped flat leaf parsley

Slice eggplants and soak in salted water. Leave for 15 minutes.

Meanwhile roast red peppers until skin is charred, place in a plastic or paper bag, close tightly and leave to cool.

Lift eggplant from water and steam slices for 10 minutes. Drain and press lightly with a clean cloth to remove liquid. Chop in 1 inch cubes and set aside. Roast cumin seeds until fragrant and grind in a mortar and pestle.

Remove skin and seeds from peppers when cool and dice. Add to eggplant. Heat oil in a frying pan and cook garlic for one minute. Tip in eggplant mixture, cumin, salt and red pepper flakes. Fry for 5 minutes, stirring occasionally. Add tomato sauce and cook until thick. Taste and adjust seasoning. Add lemon juice and parsley and serve on a flat dish. Serve warm or cold.

Spicy cauliflower fritters

A little taste of India in each bite, these cauliflower fritters are amazing, better for snacking than nuts, chips or candy. Delicious hot, I also enjoy them cold on their own, partnered with crisp vegetables as a snack, served atop a salad or as an accompaniment in my lunch bag.

1 cauliflower trimmed
¼ cup flour
3 tbsp flat leaf parsley, chopped
1 clove garlic, crushed
2 shallots or one small onion, chopped
4 egs
1 ½ tsp ground cumin
1 tsp cinnamon
½ tsp turmeric
3 pinches salt
1 tsp ground black pepper
½ olive oil

Trim cauliflower into small florets. Add to a pot of salted boiling water and simmer for 15 minutes or until soft. As it is cooking, whisk the remaining ingredients, except olive oil and parsley, in a bowl to make a batter. When cooked, drain cauliflower and set aside. Add warm cauliflower to batter and mix briskly to break it down a little. Pour olive oil in a pan and heat. When oil is very hot, drop 3 tbsp of mixture for one fritter, like you would be making a pancake. Fry in small batches, approximately 3 minutes on each side, and drain on absorbent paper. Serve hot, warm or cold.

Chili-dusted mixed nuts

We had not been dating very long when I first prepared these nuts. They are spicy and frankly delicious. Prepare some, fill a bowl and sit down on the couch to enjoy them with your guy and a movie. Watch the bowl, watch who ends up holding it, watch his fingers as they riffle through them to choose favourites, notice the slight sweat on his brow as he eats them, how he licks his fingers, whether he licks yours, if he licks his fingertips to pick up the spices in the empty bowl. It can be revealing and will tell you lots about this guy while you are dating.

1-2 tbsp olive oil
1 tbsp Mexican chili powder
1 tsp each: salt, ground coriander and curry powder
½ tsp ground cumin
¼ tsp freshly ground black pepper
Pinch of sugar
1 cup each; pecan halves, whole raw almonds, unsalted blanched peanuts

Preheat oven to 325F degrees.

In a large bowl, mix oil with all the seasonings. Add nuts and toss until well coated. Lightly grease a rimmed baking sheet with a little oil and spread nuts evenly on the sheet. Bake for 12-15 minutes on the middle rack of the oven, stirring occasionally to prevent burning.

Remove nuts from oven and cool on a separate sheet to room temperature.

Vegetable pakoras

I took an Indian cooking class one fall through the local community college. We met every Tuesday night in the home economics room of a local high school, a great pile of stone that school, all Gothic architecture and smelling of past athletic glories. You had to cross the running track to approach the front steps from the street – not a promising beginning for a cooking class. But what a time we had – we twelve refugees from offices and call centres, from banks and other classrooms, all lined up at our stoves, lovingly running rice through our fingers, hearing each other's sorrows, loves and office gossip while chopping onions, laughing riotously about dropped plates and spilled ingredients – a collection of strangers instantly friends for thirteen weeks founded firmly in curries. These pakoras were a great favourite – I ate them almost as quickly as I removed them from the oil. I still do.

2 ½ cup besan gram or chickpea flour
2 cup spinach, washed and chopped
2 medium potatoes, peeled and chopped
2 small onions, peeled and chopped
2 green chilies, chopped
1 ½ tsp salt
1 tsp red chili powder
1 cup water
Oil for frying

Make a thick batter with all the ingredients except oil. Heat oil in the skillet. Deep fry spoonfuls of the batter and turn until golden brown. Drain on paper towel. Serve hot with chutney.

Coriander chutney

The instructor of my Indian cooking class was Nina, a small, brown, displaced woman with long, cascading raven hair, galloping down her back, tiny grey hairs creeping in at her temples, hands stubbed and scarred by a journey from village, across oceans to a snow covered land, a place for a woman who never knew cold. She brought in those hands favours hidden in creases, squeezed from knuckles, kneaded and shaped by her palms! She brought fiery taste to my tongue and she taught me to laugh at the tears welling up in my eyes. She taught me hot times, hot disagreements, can be laughed away, that a pinch is as good as a measure, that sometimes you have to stick your fingers in the dish to see if it is right. Forget fear and bite. This chutney is the perfect balance to pakoras, a reason to smile while tears fill your eyes.

1 bunch fresh coriander, well washed
3-4 fresh green chilies
5 tbsp fresh lime juice
1 small onion, quartered
½ tsp salt

Wash chilies and coriander. Add coriander and onion to a blender or food processor. Blend for 2 minutes. Add chilies and lime juice. Blend till smooth, season with salt as desired. Serve with hot pakoras

Bruschetta with tomatoes and basil

I grew a garden last summer. I love the smell of the earth, of a leaf of a tomato plant when you rub it, wet feet and wet hands sparkling in the July sun when the watering is done. I had rows and rows of vegetables and herbs, basil to pluck before dinner, cucumbers lying lazily in their own shade. There is no greater glory than a tomato, ripened and full, warm from the sun, plucked and carried lovingly up to the house, washed and chopped, tossed and paired with basil. One bite taught my guy how bruschetta is intended to taste – like summer!

¾ lbs ripe tomatoes, seeded and finely chopped
2 tbsp fresh basil, finely chopped
1 tbsp olive oil
½ tsp balsamic vinegar
Coarse salt to taste
Freshly ground pepper to taste
6 slices Italian bread, lightly toasted
1 large clove garlic, halved

Place tomatoes, basil, oil, vinegar, salt and pepper in a medium bowl. Toss well to combine. Set aside for a few minutes to allow flavours to blend.

Rub toasted sides of bread with the flat sides of garlic halves. Top each slice evenly with tomato mixture, using about 2 tablespoons per slice. Garnish with chopped basil leaves if desired.

Roasted pear and butternut squash soup

This soup is a quintessential autumn soup. Dusty butternut squash, available at their best just when the first really cold winds of autumn arrive, pairs beautifully with roasted pear in this lovely soup. Step away from the regular soups and lift a spoon to this creamy soup.

2 lbs butternut squash, cut in half lengthwise and seeded
2 tbsp olive oil
2 firm but ripe Anjou or Bartlett pears, cut in half lengthwise and cored
4 cups low sodium vegetable broth
½ cup heavy whipping cream
¼ tsp nutmeg
1 tbsp sugar
salt and pepper to taste

Preheat oven to 350F degrees. Brush the flesh of the squash and pears with olive oil nd place, cut side down on a rimmed baking sheet. Roast until tender when pierced with a fork, about 30 to 35 minutes. Use a spoon to scrape out the flesh of the squash and the pears and place in the work bowl of a food processor. Discard the skins. Puree until smooth. Add 1 to 2 cups of the vegetable broth and continue processing until smooth. Pour this mixture in a four quart saucepan; add the remaining broth, cream, nutmeg and sugar. Bring to a boil and then reduce to a simmer and cook for 10 minutes. Add salt and pepper to taste. When ready to serve, ladle the soup into warmed bowls and serve immediately with warm crusty fresh bread.

Parsnip, apple & Brie soup

I have only recently begun eating parsnips. I grew up hearing about these foreign-sounding, frightful, sour face inducing vegetables, served bland and boiled, more to be endured than enjoyed. The rumours could not have been more incorrect. In this recipe, they provide the foundation to this creamy, tasty soup. Apple adds tartness and the Brie introduces a level of decadence to this unusual soup.

1 tbsp butter
1 onion, finely chopped
4 cups parsnips, peeled and chopped
2 apples, peeled and quartered
4 cups vegetable broth, low sodium
4 oz cubed Brie cheese
Salt and pepper to taste

In a large saucepan, melt butter over medium heat. Stir in onions, cook for 2 minutes stirring occasionally, until onions soften. Add parsnips, apples and broth and bring to a boil. Reduce heat, cover and simmer for 15 minutes or until tender. In a blender or food processor, in batches, puree soup until smooth. Return to saucepan and stir in cheese. Heat slowly over medium heat, stirring occasionally, just until cheese melts. Season to taste. Season with a dash of nutmeg if you wish.

If soup thickens upon standing, add more broth and reheat gently.

Pretty great weekend and as I sit down here now to write, the snow falling outside the window behind me, feels like the perfect time to tell you about it. We have a fantastic time going to our Christmas parties, both held at friend's places and both full of great friends, food and drink. So of course I am going to tell you about the food or at least my food highlights! I sampled some amazing cheeses this weekend. I don't know if you are like me or not but I adore cheese, every kind from mild to strong, soft to hard. I sampled a hard, crumbly, almost parchment coloured Spanish cheese, a great French blue cheese, a dark smoked Cheddar, a Gouda with garlic, a red marbled cheese and my perennial favourite at their place a Guinness cheddar. If you have never had go out and treat yourself. It is a cheddar cheese surrounded and enveloped in dark, thick Guinness with a dark rind on it. It tastes of aged cheddar with the earthiness of Guinness. Absolutely amazing! I also discovered the joy of espresso with a shot of Sambuca in the coffee. A rich taste that offsets nicely the light, dry biscotti we were eating with the coffee. Overall it was a great way to slow down and enjoy friends and since everywhere we went it was appetizers and finger foods, I could keep eating and not bother to count how many I had had. When you only put six or seven chocolate covered almonds in your hand to eat, if you have two or three handfuls it somehow doesn't seem like as many chocolates!

I also tried out a new soup recipe I am working on with friends on Saturday night. Bit of a flop actually. I made a sweet potato and roasted red pepper soup but when we tried it is was kind of bland. Needed something, so I am still tinkering with it. Does it need nutmeg or cinnamon to make it sweeter or should I try cayenne as was suggested and make it fiery? Or perhaps they simply don't go together and it was just a flop. Happens! Actually, happens too frequently but I like flops just as much as successes. It is all fun.

Snow is coming down outside and this weather almost always make me think of comfort food. Comfort food, comfort for us when we are feeling low, food to feed to your guy when he needs comfort, food to feed your kids to give them comfortable memories when they are adults. Food, ah glorious food, what more can I say? I think I will run, experiment with some left over soup, perfect on a snowy day, and heat up a left over stuffed pepper for dinner. Left over night around this house!

Hearty beef and vegetable soup

The key I find to good beef soup is to let go of your fear of fat. Select a rich, large beef bone or two to add to the stock. You can usually get them free from your butcher or the meat department of the grocery store or if you have to pay a few dollars, it will be worth the price. Choose beef with some fat marbled in the meat. It will melt and add flavour to the soup. Crack the bones for more flavour. Simmer slowly but for a long time. Chill and remove the fat and bones. You will be astonished by the difference it will make to your soup.

1 lb lean stewing beef, cut in 1 inch pieces
1 or 2 large beef bones
6 cups water
2 ½ cups diced tomatoes
2 cups diced potatoes
2 cups diced carrots
1 cup diced celery
1 cup diced white turnips
1 medium onion, diced
¼ cup pearl barley
6 whole cloves
1 bay leaf
¼ tsp black pepper
salt to taste

Place all ingredients in a deep kettle and cover. On high heat, raise soup to a boil. Turn heat to low and simmer for 1 ½ to 2 hours or until meat is tender. Remove bones. Chill overnight and skim off fat. Reheat and serve.

Crème Vichyssoise

I am addicted to potatoes. It must be the Irish blood running in my veins from my maternal grandmother's side. The Murphy family had a long love affair with the potato and no meal was complete without them boiled, fried, baked, mashed, at breakfast, at lunch and at dinner. I have even eaten chip butties, fries between two slices of buttered white bread. I love this easy soup, one of many potato soups, for its velvety texture and versatility. Add cheese, sour cream, onions, bacon - any combination for new flavours.

4 leeks
3 cups sliced potatoes
3 cups boiling water
4 cups low sodium chicken or vegetable broth
3 tbsp butter
1 cup light cream
1 cup milk
¼ tsp pepper
2 tbsp minced chives
¼ tsp paprika

Cut leeks with 3 inches of green tops into fine pieces and rinse well. Cook leeks and potatoes in water, covered, until tender, about 40 minutes. Press, without draining, through a fine sieve into top of double boiler. Add next 6 ingredients and stir well. Heat over hot water. Serve hot or thoroughly chilled, garnished with chives and paprika.

French onion soup

The real trick to making exceptional onion soup is first, allow the onions to cook slowly over low heat and for a long time, past that moment when you think they are done, then past that moment you think they will burn, till they are caramelized and releasing their sugars and second, always use a rich, dark beef broth and never short the pouring of the wine into the pot.

½ lb stewing beef
beef bones
2 onions, chopped
2 bay leaves
½ cup parsley sprigs
2 tsp whole black peppercorns
8 cups water
3 tbsp butter
1 tbsp olive oil
4 large onions, thinly sliced
¼ flour
¼ dry red wine
1 small French bread stick
2 tbsp butter
1 cloves garlic
¼ cup freshly grated Parmesan cheese

To make stock, combine beef, bones, chopped onions, bay leaves, parsley peppercorns and water in a large saucepan, bring stock to a boil, reduce heat, simmer gently for 3 hours. Strain, cool, refrigerate overnights. Skim fat from top of stock.

Heat butter and oil in a large sauce pan, add the sliced onions, cook over low heat until onions are golden brown and soft, about 20 minutes, stirring constantly. The longer you slowly cook the onion, the more it will caramelize. Add flour and stir over heat for 1 mine. Add wine and 5 cups of stock, stir constantly over heat until mixture boils and thickens. Reduce heat and simmer for 10 minutes.

Slice the bread. Melt extra butter, add garlic and brush onto each slice. Place on an ungreased baking sheet, bake in a moderate oven, until toasted. Top with Parmesan cheese and toast until melted. Place cheese toasts in the bottom of the bowls and top with hot soup.

I had lunch today in the lunchroom at the office. I carried my lonely little salad across the office and sat down at a table in the lunchroom. Already eating, I looked up when someone sat down at my table and, to my surprise, I had no idea who they were. By the end of hour, however, we had become fast friends. It has made me think today of university, those golden hued days of memory, of setting out for university, those lonely terrifying first weeks when you are anxiously approaching each day worrying if you will succeed at school but more so worrying whether you will find a new circle of friends, the terrifying exhilaration of living away from home for the first time, so many firsts, first year, first dorm, first friend, first groove. Today in the lunchroom I couldn't help but be reminded of the dining hall at my dorm at school. I remember those endlessly high brown brick walls, the abstract art on them, placed more to fill the space than for any artistic merit, the rows upon rows of Formica topped tables, collapsible chairs repeatedly filled by the hungry and just as quickly abandoned, forlorn until being refilled, an endless cycle of meetings and break ups, all encircling food.

Now as a food lover, the dining hall was a heavenly place for me, even if the food wasn't always first class. Our food provider was named Beaver foods, not an auspicious start to a culinary experience since typically the only beavers I came in touch with were lifeless and smashed on the side of the road. But I have to admit to falling in love with the endless parade of new dishes presented to the weary, the hungry, the aimless student class. I also came to recognize the patterns as we saddled up the trough as the semester progressed. Hip of Beef, unfortunately presented on the sign advertising it with an apostrophe leading to colloquial references to hippo beef, was Thursday's offering, breaded nondescript fish served Fridays, Monday were leftovers not so cleverly disguised as Shepherd's pie. Always there were the faithful offerings of fries with gravy, soups of last night's vegetables. While on holidays even now, I am instantly transported back to school whenever I eat a sandwich sold in a plastic triangle container. You know what I mean, a sandwich, mass produced with egg salad or tuna or roast beef and hard, processed cheese, served cut diagonally, its innards splayed forward at which the world can gawk, its crusts pointed back into the plastic corner, and then the whole thing covered in vacuum sealed see-through plastic like a window-adorned coffin with the drapes pulled aside. I ate endless sandwiches presented to me thus and that bread always had a slightly stiff texture, as though it had been embalmed with formaldehyde, a corpse of a sandwich rather than a fresh one.

But it was the companionship of that hall that amazed me. It was where you made your first friends, over a plate of spaghetti. It was the first easy place to take a roommate from your dorm or friend from class when your friendship wasn't yet strong enough for a restaurant or a movie, your uncertainty with them and your conversation was covered by the noise of the dining hall. It was a cheap first date with that special someone, a place where you could both escape from a bad date easily, where going Dutch only involved swiping your meal plan card, where again any awkward silences were covered by the din of the hall. I remember friends who I would see every day, but only ever in the dining hall, never in dorm, never class, never out of class, only in the dining hall, friends of circumstance, routine, class schedules and shared tables. But they were part of the fabric of that place, as much as grey hippo beef congealing in gravy or the constant scrape of chairs being pushed back. Today's easy conversation with a work colleague I had never met over a salad brought from home in a plastic Tupperware container reminded so strongly of the old days, when making friends was as easy as swiping your meal plan card, scraping back a chair, plopping down your plastic tray covered in food your mother would never prepare for you and launching into conversation.

Moroccan carrot soup

This remarkably simple soup is equally surprising for its full flavour and appeal. I like to prepare this soup and serve with spicy appetizers or as a palate cleanser before a subsequent dish of savoury spices. Served chilled, it partners well with green salads for a colourful starter for any outdoor summer meal.

2 lbs carrots, peeled and chopped
2 cups freshly squeezed orange juice
2 tbsp fresh lemon juice
½ tsp sugar
Pinch cardamom or ginger
Chopped fresh parsley

In a food processor, process carrots until finely chopped. Add the remaining ingredients and process until thoroughly blended. Cover and refrigerate until chilled. Serve chilled, garnished with parsley and pistachios nuts if desired.

Gazpacho

Gazpacho reminds me of holidays in the sun. Find a sun dappled patio somewhere, set a beautiful table, ladle a bowl of this heaven, garnish how you like it and enjoy the cool refreshment of this soup.

2 lbs tomatoes, peeled, chopped with juices
1 yellow bell pepper, chopped
2 red bell peppers, chopped
1 bunch green onions, chopped
1 slice stale Italian bread, soaked in water and squeezed dry
2 tbsp balsamic vinegar
2 large cloves garlic, minced
Pinch ground cumin
Pinch cayenne pepper
Salt and pepper to taste
3 tbsp olive oil

In a food processor, place tomatoes, red and yellow peppers, onions, bread, vinegar, garlic, cumin, cayenne, salt and pepper. Process until smooth and foamy. With motor running, add stream of oil till well mixed. Transfer to a large bowl, cover and refrigerate for at least 1 hour.

While soup is chilling, chop red, yellow peppers, green onions and cucumbers into tiny cubes to serve as garnishes atop the soup. Serve chilled.

Egyptian lentil soup

Whenever I make this soup I think of relationships: tears when heated can become sweet, sometimes you have to wait until the right time to add a new ingredient to the mix and that simple ingredients, like simple gestures, often produce the richest broth.

1 small red onion, thinly sliced
4 tbsp olive oil
2 medium yellow onions, coarsely chopped
½ cup carrots, chopped
1 stalk celery, chopped
2 cloves garlic, minced
1 ½ tsp cumin seeds
1 tsp fennel seeds
4 cups vegetable broth
4 cups water
1 ½ cup lentils, rinsed
Salt and pepper to taste
2 tbsp lemon juice

Preheat oven to 425F degrees. Place red onion in a pie pan and toss with 2 tbsp of olive oil. Cover pan with foil and bake 15 minutes. Remove from oven and let stand covered until ready to use.

In a large stockpot, heat remaining oil, add chopped onions, carrots, celery, garlic, cumin and fennel seeds and cook until vegetables are tender, about 15 minutes. Add the broth, water and lentils, season with salt and pepper. Bring to a boil, reduce heat, and simmer partially covered for 30 minutes. Uncover and simmer for 15 minutes more, stirring occasionally until broth has thickened slightly.

Stir in reserved red onion with oil and lemon juice. Season as necessary with salt and pepper and serve hot with lemon wedges.

Egypt, fabled land of pyramids, camels, the Nile, souks and donkeys. Egypt was the first stop on our honeymoon cruise and I was filled with anticipation to finally see the land that I had studied, imagined and re-created in my day dreams.

I just loved seeing the food in Egypt. As we would speed alongside a dusty, sluggish canal, traveling to an ancient site to see pyramids or mastaba, I was fascinated by the irrigated fields flashing by. Rows of date palms stood in orderly rows for miles like sentinels on watch. Cabbages, grain or beans lay lush between well-ordered fields, the eternal sun glinting off the water in the ditches. Groves of fruit trees shouldered against the canals, pomegranates ripening in the sun. Everywhere, I saw history living out its endless cycle. It is an ancient land filled with ancient food. Whenever we stopped to eat, I could taste the history. I was struck by the continuity of this cuisine, food that has nourished this people for over five thousand years and continues to strengthen arms and fill stomachs.

It was a land of contrasts for me. Chaotic, bustling cities filled with people bumping against each other like so many balls in a pinball machine, each bouncing from one to the next in an endless sea of movement. Quiet, eternal countryside, reminding the city dwellers of the changeless nature of Egypt, of continuity, of patience, of calm. Restaurants with cuisine from around the world, the ubiquitous Chinese restaurant, English breakfasts, French pastries, and there, nestled proudly among these visitors, rich, garlicky hummus, stewed lentils, crisp greens with chickpeas glistening atop, sticky date pastries, rich in your mouth and warm in your hands. It was for me an endless opportunity to watch trucks and donkey carts scamper past filled with dates, cabbages, grapes, pomegranates, chickens and goats, heading to markets and ultimately someone's counter in their kitchen to be transformed into the evening meal. Feeding their guy. The same eternal cycle played out in a different kitchen but animated with the same love.

Egypt, at first blush, was shocking to me, vastly different, rapid, noisy, dusty, demanding. But under the surface, I saw home. I saw the same love of food and family. The same tastes that I enjoy in restaurants were here commonplace, ancient and available. In the early mornings, the smell of warm bread often filled the air while the call to prayer sounded above the city. There was a feeling of history that seems soaked into the land and the cuisine was no different; a stew of lentils that graced the tables of nobles in pharaoh's Egypt was found for me on buffet tables and sidewalk restaurants. The food had that the flavour of time, of olive oil, dates and chickpeas, of Nile fish, lamb and fowl. Egypt that began so alien to me ended as a lesson in history, in continuity, in the power of food to define us and give us a place in our own histories.

Minestrone

I am not certain why this soup does not have the reputation of a relationship builder. Just like my experience in dating my guy, these many, unique ingredients blend as one into an immensely satisfying soup. I like to have a kettle of this soup almost always around. When he gets home first, it is reheated, ladled into bowls, salad chopped and bread sliced and dinner is waiting for me – accompanied by his welcoming smile.

1 cup white navy or cannelloni beans, drained
8 cups vegetable broth
¼ cup olive oil
2 medium onions, chopped
½ cup carrots, chopped
1 stalk celery, chopped
4 large cloves garlic, minced
1 (28 oz) can plum tomatoes, juices reserved
½ tsp dried thyme
¼ tsp ground sage
2 bay leaves
2 large potatoes, peeled and cubed
½ cup green beans, trimmed and cut in 1 inch lengths
2 cups green cabbage, shredded
½ cup elbow macaroni
2 small zucchini, cubed
2 cups baby spinach
¼ cup flat leaf parsley, chopped

In a large saucepan, heat oil, add onions, carrots, celery and cook until softened, about 10 minutes. Add garlic and cook 2 minutes. Add broth, tomatoes, thyme, sage, bay leaves, salt and pepper and bring to a boil. Reduce heat, cover and simmer for 20 minutes.

Add the potatoes, green beans, cabbage and pasta stirring well to combine. Bring to a boil, reduce heat and simmer for 10 minutes. Add zucchini and spinach and simmer for 5 minutes. Add beans and parsley, stirring well to combine. Cover, adjust heat and simmer until pasta and vegetables are tender. Serve hot.

Pasta and bean soup

This is my cold rainy day soup. This wonderfully flavourful soup is nutritious, filling and appeals to all tastes. Able to be made on a budget, this soup makes a hearty lunch or dinner, especially when partnered with bread and butter.

3 tbsp olive oil
1 medium onion, chopped
½ cup carrots, chopped
2 stalks celery, chopped
4 cloves garlic, minced
2 (28 oz) cans plum tomatoes
4 cups vegetable broth
4 cups cannelloni or navy beans, drained
¼ tsp dried thyme
¼ tsp red pepper flakes
1 bay leaf
Salt and pepper to taste
1 cup elbow macaroni
¼ cup fresh basil, chopped
¼ cup fresh flat leaf parsley, chopped

In a large saucepan, heat the oil over medium heat. Add onions, carrots, celery and garlic and cook until softened, about 5 minutes. Add tomatoes and their liquid, broth, beans, thyme, red pepper flakes, bay leaf salt and pepper and bring to a boil. Reduce heat and simmer uncovered for 15 minutes, stirring occasionally.

Add the pasta and bring to a boil. Reduce heat to medium and simmer for 10 minutes. Reduce heat to low and add basil and parsley, stirring until just wilted. Serve hot.

Curried quinoa salad

Quinoa has emerged as the super grain of the Andes, packed with protein and terribly versatile. Served over a bed of fresh lettuce, this salad has many textures to delight the tongue and is hearty enough to be meal unto itself.

1 cup quinoa
2 ½ cup vegetable broth
½ cup walnut pieces
½ cup shredded carrots
3 green onions, sliced
¼ cup chopped cilantro
¾ cup dried apricots, chopped finely
½ cup dried cranberries
1 tbsp canola oil

Dressing:

2 tbsp curry powder
¼ cup freshly squeezed lime juice
1 tbsp honey
¼ cup canola oil

Place the quinoa in a sieve and rinse thoroughly, perhaps two or three times. Drain and place in a medium saucepan, along with the broth. Bring to a boil. Cover, reduce heat and simmer until all the liquid is absorbed, about 10 to 15 minutes. Remove from heat, fluff with a fork and set aside.

While quinoa is simmering, preheat the oven to 350F degrees. Place walnut pieces on a baking sheet and toast until golden brown and fragrant, about 8 to 10 minutes. In a large bowl, combine carrots, green onions, cilantro, apricots, toasted walnut pieces, cranberries and cooked quinoa.

For dressing, mix curry powder, lime juice, honey and canola oil in a sealable container; shake well to mix. Pour over the quinoa mixture and toss together. Refrigerate the salad at least one hour. Toss again and serve.

Tuna chickpea salad

This salad is a carryover from my university days. It is delicious and easy. I made it one day for my lunch while my guy was sniffing around the kitchen to see what I was doing. One spoonful sold him and now we both often take it for lunch to work in Tupperware. It is filling and the proteins in the fish and the beans keep you feeling satisfied all afternoon.

2 14 oz cans chickpeas
1 can white tuna
3 green onions, diced
¼ cup olive oil
2 fresh lemons
½ tsp oregano
Pinch of salt

Drain and rinse the chickpeas in a sieve and put in a mixing bowl. Flake and add tuna to chickpeas, add green onions, olive oil, oregano and salt. Mix well. Squeeze lemon juice including pulp (but not the seeds!) into the salad and mix well. Taste. You can adjust the lemon or the oil depending on your preference. Let marinate in the fridge for an hour. Always serve at room temperature to prevent the oil from solidifying.

Easiest marinated vegetable salad ever

It has become somewhat of a tradition in my family that I prepare and take this salad to any family gathering in addition to whatever else I may be bringing. It has taken on its own myth, this signature salad – though there is nothing signature particularly about it. In fact, it was my mother's recipe originally but somehow it has become associated almost exclusively with me. That happens sometimes with recipes – just honour who gave it to you and continue preparing it for everyone to enjoy.

16 baby carrots, cut lengthwise
1 head broccoli, cut in florets
1 head cauliflower, cut in florets
1 small red onion, quartered and sliced thinly
1 each red, yellow and orange pepper, coarsely chopped
1 pint red grape tomatoes
1 small cucumber, cut lengthwise, coarsely chopped
1 bottle fat free Italian salad dressing

Wash, cut and prepare the carrots, broccoli and cauliflower into bite-size pieces. Place vegetables in a large bowl. Pour the entire bottle of salad dressing over the vegetables. Toss and coat. Cover the bowl and refrigerate overnight, mixing the vegetables occasionally. The next day, add the red onion, peppers, tomatoes and cucumber and toss to coat. Refrigerate and marinate for 4 hours, stirring occasionally.

Orange, pineapple jellied salad

This salad is a favourite of my younger brother. Popular in the late seventies, this salad would often grace our table as children in the summer. I could not imagine summer picnics or barbeques at home or at my grandparents' without it nestled squarely between potato salad, cold ham and devilled eggs, radish roses floating in water and cucumber slices in vinegar, us kids running on the green lawn beneath leafy maples, us kids carousing, all legs and arms and curly blond hair streaming behind us, being called to lunch and my brother, his freckles fresh, his red hair shining, racing for his favourite bowl, the first with the spoon.

1 14 oz can of pineapple chunks, drained
1 can mandarin oranges, drained
1 package orange Jello
1 can frozen orange juice concentrate
1 cup boiling water

In a large bowl, dissolve the Jello in the boiling water. Once dissolved, add the fruit and the frozen orange juice and stir until completely combined. Refrigerate, stirring occasionally to ensure that the fruit does not settle on the bottom of the bowl.

Grilled chicken salad

Everyone knows how to prepare a grilled chicken salad. Here is my version. I enjoy the pairing of peaches and pears with chicken and greens. This salad always makes the job of preparing a light supper or lunch easy.

12 oz boneless, skinless chicken breasts
3 tbsp olive oil
2 tbsp fresh lime juice
1 clove garlic, minced
4 cups salad greens
3 green onions, chopped
1 peach, pitted and sliced
1 pear, cored and sliced
2 tbsp cilantro, chopped
3 tbsp low fat Italian salad dressing

In a shallow glass dish, arrange chicken in a single layer. In a small bowl, stir together olive oil, lime juice and garlic and pour over chicken. Cover and refrigerate for 30 minutes or up to 4 hours.

Discard marinade. Place chicken on a greased grill over medium-high heat. Close lid and grill, turning once, until no longer pink inside, about 12 to 15 minutes. Let rest for 5 minutes and slice into strips.

In a large salad bowl, toss together salad greens, green onions, peach and pear slices, and cilantro and chicken strips. Drizzle with salad dressing to moisten and toss again. Serve.

Caesar salad with homemade croutons

Do not be afraid to make this recipe; Caesar salad is really easy to make from scratch. But do use a wooden bowl. If you do not have one, buy one. It makes all the difference. You need the roughness in the bowl to grind the ingredients. If you use anything less than three cloves of fresh garlic, I will not admit to this recipe. Remember if he will kiss you with garlic breath then he is the guy for you.

3 thick slices of stale sourdough or rustic bread, cut into ¾ inch cubes
3 tbsp olive oil
¼ tsp salt
1 tsp coarsely ground black pepper
3 cloves garlic, minced or more
2 anchovies or 1 tsp anchovy paste
2 tsp Dijon mustard
1 egg yolk, coddled
1 ½ tsp freshly squeezed lemon juice
1 tsp Worcestershire sauce
¼ cup safflower or light olive oil
1 ½ tsp red wine vinegar
large head of romaine lettuce, washed and thoroughly dried
½ cup grated Parmesan cheese

To make croutons, preheat oven to 350F degrees. Place the bread in a large bowl and add olive oil. Toss and squish the bread like a sponge until the oil is evenly absorbed. Place the crouton on a baking sheet or aluminum foil and bake in the oven for about 20 minutes or until golden brown.

Start the dressing by adding salt and pepper to the salad bowl. Add the garlic. Using the back of a soupspoon, grind the garlic against the wall of the bowl until well mashed. Add the anchovies and once again using the spoon grind into a paste.

Follow the same procedure adding the Dijon, egg yolk, lemon juice and Worcestershire sauce one at a time. Ensure that each ingredient is blended into a smooth paste with the previous ingredients before proceeding. Add the oil and vinegar. Blend well.

Just before serving, tear the lettuce leaves into bite sized pieces and add to the salad bowl. Toss thoroughly with dressing. Add the croutons and cheese, toss again and serve immediately.

On my way to work this morning, I was thinking about perseverance. When I was around seven or eight years old, we lived for a few years in a small, country village called Inglewood. It was a quiet place, nestled amid rolling country hills, a small town with a church, a corner store to buy candy, a post office, a skating arena and not much else. It was an ideal place to grow up, safe, lots of wild places to explore, great hills to ride your sleigh down, a place where you could walk to Sunday school alone. I remember one autumn day getting a phone call from my mother. She had been out, not sure where, telling me that our trusty, old green car had broken down on the highway and she was walking back home. She asked that I take a set of old, abandoned rail tracks through the fields and meet her halfway. I readily set out on what felt like an adventure.

I remember walking through the fields on the old rail bed, quite pleased. I have always enjoyed walking and particularly enjoy walking in the country. I do, however, remember very clearly coming to a train trestle along the rail bed. Walking up to the flat rails passing over a small stream, the day turned cold. Looking back, I am sure the channel was no more than eight feet deep, but at the time, it was a chasm to me. I am paralyzed by heights, deathly afraid. Stretching out ahead of me were the black, railroad ties, like a scar on the countryside, light shining up between the yawning gaps between them. I remember the yellowing weeds in the ditch, the last purple cornflowers and browning golden rod. I stood there.

I had promised to meet my mother, walking toward me. I swallowed. My hands started to sweat. My feet went cold. I placed my running shoe on the first tie, my white shoes stark against the black tar-stained tie. I swung my foot to meet its mate. I stood. I shivered. I looked down and away. I reached out and placed my foot on the second tie and swung its waiting mate. Slowly, one tie at a time, this is how I crossed the trestle, never looking down, eyes firmly fixed on the horizon. In a blink I was across and a great whoosh of breath left me and a burden was lifted from my shoulders. I walked light hearted the rest of the way and, seeing Mom in the distance coming toward me, I had kept my promise.

I will remember those yawning, black timbers and, today, place my foot firmly on the first one. I have to remember to keep my promises, especially to myself, and keep going.

Cucumber and tomato salad

When you need a fast, delicious, easy to prepare salad, this one is a great choice. It uses only the freshest ingredients, can be prepared in moments, adjusted to your taste, contains no fat and the combination of lemon and lime juices gives it a playful snap. Enjoy it anytime but especially on warm summer evenings al fresco with grilled meats and a nice glass of wine.

4 large tomatoes, seeded and chopped
1 large cucumber, chopped
1 large red onion, chopped
½ cup fresh mint leaves, finely chopped
½ cup flat leaf parsley, finely chopped
1 bunch green onions, chopped
2 large cloves garlic, minced
3 tbsp olive oil
2 tbsp fresh lemon juice
1 ½ tbsp fresh lime juice
Salt and pepper to taste

In a large bowl, place all ingredients, tossing well to combine. Let stand at room temperature for 15 minutes to let flavours blend. Toss again and serve.

I was eighteen when I left home for university, a young eighteen. Having grown up in the country, when I arrived at university in the city, I had never ridden a city bus, been in a taxi, lived in apartment or even eaten Chinese food. Everything was brand new to me.

While at school, I made friends with an older student in my Greek literature class. Looking back, she probably wasn't even as old as I am now but, at the time, she was a mature student. Christina, whose nickname was Soula, was Greek by heritage and soon became a close and trusted friend, despite our age difference. It was through Soula that I had my first taste of a cuisine from a culture other than my own. I suppose I ate spaghetti and lasagna as a child but I would hardly typify those samplings as Italian food and so Soula's Greek food had the feel of the exotic to me. I can remember distinctly my apartment at school and how we would, late in the afternoon, after classes had finished, return to my kitchen and prepare garlicky pork roasts or simple chicken soups, flavoured with lemon and fresh eggs whipped into them. In particular, I remember the tomatoes.

Regularly, Soula would turn up with a bag of bursting ripe, red tomatoes from her garden, a firm, cool cucumber, a sweet red onion. Into a large bowl, we would chop them up, the tomatoes spilling their juices across the bottom of the bowl. With some olives, oil, cheese and seasoning, we would let this salad sit in the sun on the counter by the fridge and let the juices marinate. Salt would tease more juice from the tomatoes till the bottom half of the salad was swimming. We would carry the whole bowl into my front living room, where we would often sit on my plush green shag carpet, forgoing the luxuries of my hand-me-down orange couch without legs. We would break apart a large loaf of crusty bread and, each of us armed with a fork would enjoy the salad directly from the bowl.

When we could reach it, we would dip chunks of bread into the tomato juices, soaking up the summer sun and the reflected sun of the Aegean that nourished the olives and the oregano, lifting these delicious morsels to our mouths, tomato juice running down our arms. We would eat the whole bowl this way, talking about virtues of the Aeneid or the differences between Doric or Corinthian columns. All my memories of both my degrees seem to be framed around food. And here I have come full circle. My instruction manual on InDesign to lay out this cookbook has arrived and thinking about tomatoes reminded me that I am able to learn when I put my mind to it. And I am motivated knowing that at the end, there will be a good meal waiting. I better run, time to prepare dinner.

Romaine, red onion and chickpea salad with orange vinaigrette

Almost every day, I dutifully pack in my trusty Tupperware a salad for my lunch at my desk. Like a lonely, grey, heavy laden worker, chained to the walls of my cubicle, pecking at my computer like that ubiquitous chicken pecking piano keys in hopes of a tube full of grain. But at lunch, I reach for this salad, its freshness and tastes bringing light to my office, like the sun peeking from behind a cloud.

¼ cup fresh orange juice
4 tsp olive oil
1 tbsp fresh lemon juice
1 clove garlic, minced
Salt and pepper to taste
1 (19 oz) can chickpeas, washed and drained
1 small red onion, peeled, quartered, thinly sliced
8 cups torn romaine leaves, washed and dried

Soak red onion in cold water for 10 minutes, remove, and drain. In a medium bowl, whisk together orange juice, oil, lemon juice, garlic, salt and pepper. Add the chickpeas and onion. Toss well to combine. Let stand for 15 minutes to allow flavours to blend. Toss again.

Divide lettuce leaves on plates and spoon chickpea mixture evenly over the lettuce. Serve at room temperature.

Spinach and orange salad with pine nuts and raisins

This is one of my favourites and frequently shows up on my plate. Even my guy enjoys this salad and he frequently adds strawberries and blueberries to the salad. Pairing oranges with spinach aids your body in absorbing the iron from the spinach.

8 cups baby spinach, washed and dried
2 large oranges, peeled, cut into rounds
½ cup pine nuts, toasted
½ cup raisins, soaked in warm water, drained
¼ cup olive oil
2 tbsp fresh orange juice
2 tbsp sherry vinegar
Salt and pepper to taste

In a large salad bowl, combine spinach, oranges, pine nuts and raisins. In a small bowl, whisk together oil, juice, vinegar, salt and pepper until well blended. Add to the spinach mixture and toss gently but thoroughly until combined. Serve at once.

Bread salad

When I was in Australia, I was invited to lunch with good friends. Sitting down to a Lebanese meal of barbequed chicken, toum, tabbouleh, and hummus was a special treat. This salad accompanied the meal – it was love at first sight. A fresh salad full of diverse flavours with the added crunch of toasted bread, this one could quickly become a favourite.

2 medium day old pitas
1 large clove garlic, halved
2 tbsp olive oil, plus 1 tsp olive oil
2 tomatoes, chopped
1 cup red onion, chopped
1 cucumber, chopped
¼ cup flat leaf parsley, chopped
2 tbsp fresh mint, chopped
2 tbsp fresh lemon juice
Salt and pepper to taste
4 cups mixed greens or lettuce, washed and dried

Preheat oven to broil. Separate each pita into halves; rub the flat sides of pita with garlic. Arrange the bread on a baking sheet and brush tops with a teaspoon of olive oil. Broil until toasted for about 1-2 minutes. Set aside.

Place tomatoes, onion, cucumber, parsley, mint, lemon juice and remaining oil in a large bowl. Add garlic. Season with salt and pepper and toss to combine. Set aside for 15 minutes, then toss again.

Break toasted pita into bite size pieces. Just before serving, combine pitas and lettuce in a large serving bowl. Add the tomato mixture and toss well to combine. Serve at once.

Just a quick laugh, mostly tongue in cheek but perhaps also a little too true. Do you want to know exactly how much you love your guy, then offer to peel and de-seed a pomegranate for him! I love pomegranates and it has become a tradition for my guy and me to enjoy them at this time of year. But truly, standing in the kitchen de-seeding a pomegranate is like going through all the phases of dating and a relationship in the time it takes to prepare one! You start off looking at it, admiring its rosy colour, its soft roundness, wondering where it came from and how it made its journey to you. You cut into it and it sprays sweet juice all over the counter and your hands, giving you a chance to slowly lick your fingers and taste its promise. And then the work begins. You peel back the first layers of skin, exposing the seeds, but somehow you are always on the wrong side of the row. You have to turn it around, and push them out with your fingers. You start to get a rhythm only to come across a particularly thick-skinned area. You start to get frustrated, wondering why you ever started. You try not to glance at the other half sitting on the counter waiting its turn. You back starts to twinge standing on the tile floor. You recommit and keep at it. You just focus on finding the right way to peel it. One half done and you pick up the other piece. You have learned how this one is set up and know where to attack the rows first. This half seems easier; it is more familiar. You don't notice the time you are expending and somehow your back eases. The bowl is starting to look full and you feel a sense of satisfaction at your progress. You remember why you started, why you wanted to share it with your guy. You are in the home stretch suddenly and you start to anticipate sharing the bowl together, your hands covered in a familiar sweet stickiness now, the bowl overflowing with promise. You rinse your hands to say you are done. Put two spoons in the bowl and walk to the living room to share the pomegranate, a smile on your face. And you know you love him when he insists you take the first delicious spoonful.

Going steady

They say the way to man's heart is through his stomach. I wanted to test the truth of this old saying. Fortunately, I also love to cook so it was a double-sided pleasure.

As our dates progressed, we became more serious, as I suppose we all do, almost without noticing. I am perhaps more unconscious than most, never taking close account of my actions, of how my actions speak more clearly of my intentions and of my feelings than I would ever let on.

I remember my first grocery list that I jotted down with my guy in mind. Suddenly, I was taking into account someone else's tastes and preferences, dislikes and favourites. I remember when I started altering his diet.

When I met my guy, he ate much like a monk, sparingly, hastily and with a great deal of repetition. Meals at his place had a certain predictability to them, a sameness that tasted like bachelorhood. A beautiful fridge fill only with condiments, cupboards filled with excess dishes for a man who used only one plate and one glass, a desert of lingering smells of last week's dinners repeated in an endless cycle, prepared this week and stretching forward in a mist of smells to come. My guy enjoyed his food and eating with company. Enough shared plates of steamed dumplings in Chinatown or plates of wings and beer over pool demonstrated to me his love of food.

Into this land of culinary opportunity I walked. I began slowly, making the recipes that follow, having a meal ready for us. I began to cherish those last thirty minutes before he came home, the smell of dinner filling the air, the wine open, the table set, languidly wiping down the counters or washing a dish, alone in the house, the air expectant, lighting candles or slicing fruit for garnish. Eventually I was able to name that feeling: contentment.

Then my guy would arrive home, loud and rushing in the door, work bag thrown upon the floor, kicking off his shoes and slouching out of his coat, calling for the kettle to be put on for a tea. Then my favourite moment, when he would walk into the kitchen and be arrested in mid-stride – his smiling face, a kiss for me, and then, always, lifting a lid or opening an oven door, peering inside and sighing. Dinner would follow and the day's stories would spill from both our lips as wine was drunk and plates cleared. Our life was being built, in little moments, plate by plate, at our little table.

I have always insisted that we eat together at the table, no matter how simple the meal, how rushed the time, how tired we are. It is our gathering place. It reminds us to slow down, to see each other, to show gratitude for the food we have, give thanks for our blessings and thanks for the preparation of the meal. It reminds us to talk to each other, to take the time to remember each other's faces. No matter how busy the day or how crazy, difficult or demanding the world was of us that day, our table is one of peace and comfort. I know the appeal of dinner in front of the television but it is our table that grounds us.

As our relationship grew more serious, it was that grounding upon which we built our future. I remember our first disagreements, fights even, those stomach-wrenching sweats, and the fear, and the hurt and yet somehow, a meal would show me if we had reconciled. It is difficult to sit at your table, the meal prepared and shared, and not find yourself putting your fork down to talk honestly and find resolution. Food like ashes on your tongue before became sweet again after talking and hopefully dessert would be forgotten for other pleasures.

Going steady is about learning and compromising, shared experience and laughter. It is also about routine, trust and ordinary life: laundry and dishes, groceries and errands, birthdays, holidays and anniversaries.

Cooking, when I am conscious and thoughtful about it, teaches me how to care for the man I love. When I am impatient with him or myself, I produce a flop. I have to learn to ask for help, to follow direction and ask for clarification. I have to think ahead and plan. I need to consider another. I am responsible for another's physical health. I influence his emotional health. I foster communication or stop it. I can learn to laugh at mistakes and know how it feels to stand unembarrassed in front of someone when it all goes wrong. Cooking shows me what kind of life I am creating, how adventurous I can be, how dependable, how loving. Cooking made me pay attention to the type of person I was in our relationship – and if I did not like the taste, then I had better adjust the seasonings.

Going steady and feeding my guy became wrapped up in one. Going steady is the main meal. These meals are a commitment to him and a revelation to you. Let them slow you down, enjoy preparing and sharing them, serve each dish as an event at your own little table, laugh over them, talk over them, share the burdens of the day and dream plans for the future over them. Put your fork down occasionally to caress his face or refill your wine glass. Lean back in your chair and just look at him, listen to his day, knowing he is telling you, eating your food, being nourished by your love. The main meal is life – enjoy it.

Beef and cheddar Brats with beer-braised onions

Going steady is the meat of your relationship, a kind of trial run before marriage, a period of learning and accommodating and dreaming. This is the time of first steps in providing a pure and nourishing diet for you both, when you can create for yourselves a diet both beneficial and loved by both, avoiding things injurious to your health. This recipe finds a happy balance between joy of food and drink and wholesomeness.

4 tbsp butter
2 red onions, thinly sliced
1 yellow onion, thinly sliced
1 bottle of dark ale or stout
8 beef and cheddar Bratwurst sausages
8 dark rye rolls
Stone-ground mustard

Set up grill for direct cooking over high heat. Oil grill grate when ready to start cooking.

Place a large skillet on a grill or side burner and add butter. When butter has melted, add onions. Cook until softened, about 10 minutes. Add beer and cover. Cook for an additional 10 minutes.

Remove cover from skillet and let simmer until most of the liquid has evaporated, about 5 minutes.

Turn the heat on the grill down to medium. Place brats on oiled grill grates and cook 4 to 5 minutes per side.

Serve sausages hot on toasted rolls smothered with onions and topped with mustard.

Irish beef and Guinness stew

This stew has become a favourite. I first made it the night before leaving on a cruise of the Mediterranean for my birthday for family and friends accompanying us. It was the first occasion my guy vacationed with my family. Our vacation was much like this stew, joyful, memorable and worth the wait.

2 lbs stewing beef, trimmed and cut into cubes
3 tbsp olive oil
2 tbsp flour
salt and pepper to taste
pinch cayenne
2 large white onions, chopped
1 clove garlic, crushed
2 tbsp tomato paste
¼ cup warm water
2 cup carrots, peeled and chopped
1 cup parsnips, peeled and chopped
1 fresh thyme sprig

Preheat oven to 275F degrees.

Dissolve tomato paste in warm water. Set aside. Toss the meat with 1 tbsp of oil to coat. In a separate bowl, mix flour, cayenne, salt and pepper. Toss the meat in the flour mixture to coat thoroughly. Heat the remaining oil in a large skillet over medium-high heat. When oil is hot, add beef in batches, browning on all sides. Ensure all beef is returned to skillet before proceeding. Reduce heat and add onions, garlic and tomato paste. Cover the skillet and cook gently for 5 minutes.

Transfer meat to a large casserole with a slotted spoon. Pour half the Guinness into the skillet. Bring to a boil and stir to dissolve the caramelized meat juices from the pan. Pour over meat along with the remaining Guinness. Add carrot, parsnip and thyme to the casserole dish, stirring gently. Adjust seasoning to taste. Cover the casserole dish and bake slowly for 2 to 3 hours or until meat is tender. Serve with garlic mashed potatoes.

Grilled steak with dark ale and mustard sauce

Dark ale and mustard combine in this presentation to add a certain depth to your enjoyment of steak. Remind your guy of the pleasures of work and wealth with this simple dish – it speaks of wealth on a shoestring budget. Find opportunities together to enjoy a measure of unrestraint mid-week.

1 ¼ cup beef stock
4 strip loin or tenderloin steaks, 6-8 oz each
¼ tsp cracked black pepper
¼ tsp fresh rosemary, chopped
½ tsp olive oil
¼ cup dark ale
1 tsp green peppercorns
2 tsp Dijon mustard
1 tsp butter, cold
½ tsp sea salt
½ tsp ground black pepper

Place the stock in a small saucepan over high heat. Cook until reduced by half. Set aside.

Season the steaks with cracked pepper and rosemary. Heat a large heavy frying pan over high heat. Once hot, add and beef; sear steaks on all sides. Remove steaks from pan and set aside.

Deglaze the pan with dark ale. Add the reduced stock and green peppercorns, cooking on high heat until sauce is reduced to half. Remove from heat and whisk in the mustard and butter. Adjust seasoning with salt and pepper if desired.

Preheat grill to high heat. Grill steaks to desired doneness and top with warmed sauce.

Spicy garlic bok choy stir fry

This recipe is a quick and easy solution for a Wednesday night, or any night when you have arrived home, frazzled by traffic, burdened by work, dragged down by children on each side pleading for dinner. This recipe prepares even more quickly with your guy at your side helping.

2 tbsp canola oil
12 oz boneless beef grilling steak, cut across grain in thin strips
12 oz baby bok choy, sliced in half lengthwise
2 cloves garlic, minced
4 oz sugar snap or snow peas
1 carrot, shredded
1/3 cup water

Sauce

1/3 cup low sodium vegetable broth
3 tbsp oyster sauce
1 tbsp low sodium soy sauce
1 tbsp cornstarch
2 tsp Asian chili garlic sauce
1 tsp sesame oil

Sauce: In a bowl, whisk together broth, oyster and soy sauces, cornstarch, chili garlic sauce and sesame oil. Set aside.

In a wok or lard deep skillet, heat tbsp of oil over high heat. Stir fry beef in two batches for two minutes or until browned but still pink inside. Transfer to a bowl. In wok, stir in remaining oil and add bok choy and garlic for two minutes. Add peas and 1/3 cup water, cover with lid and sir occasionally for three minutes or until vegetables are tender-crisp.

Pour sauce into wok, stir fry for one minute or until sauce thickens. Stir in beef and juices and stir fry for one minute. Add carrot and serve.

Cuban ropa vieja

A good friend of mine gave me this recipe. Originally from Cuba, she seems to be unable to worry, always able to see the light side, the truly absurd side of life and laugh at its appearance. Ropa vieja means old clothes in Spanish. This meat is cooked, shredded like rags and then briefly cooked again which gives it the Spanish name. How Cuban to laugh at a dish that takes steak and finally serves it in rags.

2 lbs flank steak
2 medium onions
1 carrot, coarsely chopped
1 celery stalk, coarsely chopped
1 bay leaf
2 tbsp olive oil
2 cloves garlic, minced
2 green bell peppers, chopped
1 cup fresh plum tomatoes, seeded and chopped
2 tsp dried oregano
½ tsp cumin
¼ cup parsley, chopped

Quarter one of the two onions. Put in a 6 quart kettle with meat, carrot, celery and bay leaf. Cover with water by 2 inches. Bring to a simmer and cook, uncovered, for 1 ½ to 2 hours. Skim frequently.

When meat is very tender, remove from broth. Set aside. Discard vegetables and stain broth through a sieve. Return broth to heat and boil to reduce to half, about 20 to 30 minutes. When meat is cool, cut off any fat and pull into shreds about 2 inches wide.

While broth is reducing, coarsely chopped the second onion. Heat oil in a large skillet. Over medium heat, cook onions, garlic and green peppers until softened about 10 minutes. Stir in 1 ½ cups reduced broth and tomatoes.

Cook for 15 to 20 minutes over medium heat. Stir in shredded meat, oregano, parsley and cumin. Cook 10 to 15 minutes more.

Boeuf Bourguignon

If you are single or simply want to remind your guy why he comes home each night to you, prepare this timeless stew and no guy, no man, however affected by wanderlust, distracted or undecided he may be, will leave your side. This stew is so good he will ask for it regularly and his thanks and sighs of pleasure will reward your efforts.

4-5 lbs rib steak
2 tbsp butter
2 tbsp brandy
½ cup baby mushrooms
½ cup baby onions
1 tbsp butter, extra
2 cups dry red wine
1 cup port
1 cup water
½ cup canned tomato puree
1 bay leaves
2 tbsp corn flour or cornstarch

Cut steak into large cubes. Heat butter in a large frying pan, add steak to pan in small quantities, cook stirring over heat until well browned all over. Remove steak as it is brown. When done, return all steak to the pan, add brandy, flame brandy, when flame has subsided, remove steak.

Remove stalks from mushrooms, remove skins from onions, add whole mushrooms and onions to pan with extra butter, cook for 2 minutes, remove mushroom and onions from pan.

Return steak to pan, add wine, port, half the water, tomato puree and bay leaves. Bring to a boil, reduce heat, covered and simmer for 1 hour or until steak is tender.

Add mushrooms and onions to pan, cook uncovered for 30. Remove bay leaves. Stir in corn flour blended with remaining water, stir constantly over heat until mixture boils and thickens. Serve hot.

Lamb pot

On a cold winter afternoon, snow falling outdoors, warmth in your fireplace, alone together, forgetting about the world, snug in your home, nothing satisfies like this lamb casserole served with a green salad and crusty, hot dinner rolls.

1 tbsp oil
1 tbsp butter
6 lamb chops
1 onion, chopped
2 cloves garlic, crushed
1/3 cup flour
4 cups chicken stock
1/3 cup dry red wine
2 tbsp tomato paste
1 large sprig fresh rosemary
2 tsp fresh thyme leaves or ½ tsp dried
½ cup green beans
2 sticks celery
½ cup baby carrots

Heat oil and butter in frying pan, add chops, fry on both sides till brown, remove from pan. Add onion and garlic to pan, stir constantly until onion is browned. Add flour, stir over heat. Stir in stock, wine and tomato paste, stir constantly over heat until mixture boils and thickens. Add rosemary and thyme, reduce heat and simmer 3 minutes.

Preheat oven to 350F degrees. Top and tail green beans, cut beans in half, slice and half celery. Combine chops, beans, celery and carrots in a large ovenproof dish, top with sauce, cover and bake in oven for about 1 ½ hours or until lamb is tender.

Spicy lamb curry with yoghurt and apple

I really like this recipe because the curry cooks in its own juices, marinating and tenderizing in the oven, slowly simmering, giving it a complex taste when it is finished. It can also be prepared ahead and forgotten about all afternoon – except the tantalizing smells will keep you returning to lift the lid and have a peek.

3 tbsp olive oil
3 lbs lamb shoulder, cubed, trimmed
2 onions, halved, thinly sliced
3 cloves garlic, minced
2 tsp ginger, freshly grated
1 tbsp ground cumin
1 tbsp ground coriander
1 tsp turmeric
2 cinnamon sticks
1 green chili, seeded, finely chopped
½ cup thick yoghurt
1 green apple, cored and grated
2 cups water
Sea salt
Freshly ground pepper

Preheat oven to 300F degrees.

Heat half the oil in a casserole dish with lid over high heat. Add lamb in batches and cook for 2 minutes on each side or until well browned. Remove from pan and set aside.

Reduce heat to medium and add remaining oil and onion to the pan. Cook for 5 minutes, stirring occasionally, until onion is translucent. Add garlic and ginger and cook for 1 minute longer, then add cumin, coriander, turmeric, cinnamon and chili. Cook for 2 minutes, stirring occasionally.

Return lamb to the casserole with the yoghurt, apple and water and stir to combine. Remove from heat, cover with lid and place in oven for 2 hours. Season to taste and serve with steamed couscous or basmati rice.

Chicken pot pie

For me, a large part of being in a committed relationship with my guy is about acquiring and building our knowledge of each other, finding happiness and harmony by mutual love and true respect. Never underestimate contentment – it is a rare gift, a warm, comforting security that fills your days with ease.

Pie pastry
¼ cup butter
1 small onion, diced
1 small leek, white part only, washed and chopped
1 ½ lbs boneless, skinless chicken breasts or thighs, cut into cubes
1 tsp black pepper
2/3 cup white mushrooms, cleaned and halved
¼ cup flour
1 cup dry white wine
1 cup whipping cream
¾ up whole milk
1 ½ tsp fresh thyme leaves, chopped

Preheat oven to 350F degrees.

In a large saucepan over medium heat, melt the butter. Add onion and leek and cook until translucent, about 5 minutes. Add chicken and pepper and continue to cook, stirring often, until the chicken is about half cooked but not browning. Add mushrooms and cook for a further 5 minutes. Sprinkle with flour and cook for 2-3 minutes (the mixture will be very dry). Add the wine and simmer until the wine is reduced by one quarter. Add cream, milk and thyme. Reduce heat and continue to cook until chicken is fully cooked.

Roll out pastry and line a pie pan. Pour chicken filling into pie shell. Roll out top, wet edges, place top pastry over bottom, press edges and flute or crimp. Cut a slit or leaf pattern in top to allow steam to escape. Bake for 30 minutes or until pastry is golden brown on top.

Broiled barbeque chicken wings

Game night has always been a mystery to me, a male ritual involving sports, beer, food and good-natured bickering over the merits of teams, supported by reams of statistics seemingly plucked from the air. Men cannot seem to remember the goals of an errand on which they have been sent but can remember the minutiae of sport statistics. Do not try to understand it. Support game nights and allow him to play. Serve him delicious food and be there in spirit.

16 to 20 chicken wings
2 tbsp prepared mustard
¼ cider vinegar
¾ ketchup
½ cup molasses
2 tbsp canola oil
2 tsp Worcestershire sauce
¼ tsp garlic powder
¼ tsp Tabasco sauce

Wash chicken wings and pat dry. Cut off and discard chicken wing tips; cut each wing in half at the joint. Preheat broiler and oil broiler pan. Line inside of broiler pan with foil to catch drips. Arrange chicken wings on broiler pan. Combine remaining ingredients; blending well. Remove about 1/3 cup of the sauce and refrigerate until serving time. Set aside remaining sauce for basting. Broil chicken wings about 6 inches from heat for 15 minutes, turning frequently to keep them from burning. Brush wings with sauce; turn and brush the other side. Continue broiling and basting for 10 to 15 minutes longer, removing smaller, flatter pieces earlier as needed.

Bourbon chicken wings

Try these wings for another twist on game night. They have a slightly tangy, smoky flavour and taste particularly good with a cold beer. Plates of hot wings, dips, cheese and crackers and stuffed potatoes can round out a coffee table feast of food to accompany the game. These wings will guarantee you will be invited to join the party; whether you choose to do so is up to you.

24 chicken wings
3 tbsp bourbon
3 tbsp olive oil
1 tbsp finely grated lemon peel
Juice of one lemon
1 cup fine, dry, unseasoned bread crumbs
1 tbsp sweet paprika
Salt and pepper to taste

Cut chicken wings at joints; discard tips or reserve for broth or stock. Combine the wing joints, bourbon, olive oil, lemon rind, and lemon juice in a bowl. Toss to coat the wings and marinate refrigerated for 4 hours or overnight. Mix the bread crumbs, paprika, salt, and pepper in a plastic bag. Drain the wing joints and toss with the bread crumb mixture. Place the wings on a baking sheet and place about 4 to 5 inches from heat source under preheated broiler. Broil until crisp and golden, about 5 minutes on each side.

Chicken biryani

This dish always reminds me of celebrations. India is on my wish list for future vacations and whenever I prepare this dish I am transported there, a world rich in vibrant colours, jostling activity, dust, life, sweat, wafting smells, riotous flowers and delicious food. When you prepare this dish, take a dream vacation for yourself, be transported away from home, cares, children, office and responsibilities and fly away for some adventure. They need never know where you have been when you finally place the food on the table.

4 to 5 lbs boneless chicken
3 tbsp fried onions
3 tbsp plain yoghurt
2 tsp red chili
½ tsp tumeric
2 tsp salt
1 tsp black cumin seeds
2 tbsp olive oil
2 tsp garam masala

Mix the above ingredients and marinate the chicken in a big pot for two hours.

Next place 3 cups of rice in boiling water and remove from heat. Leave rice in water until the rice becomes soft to touch then drain off water.

Place the pot of the marinated chicken on the stove on medium heat and pour the soaked rice on top of the chicken. Top the rice with a bit of orange rind and add ½ cup of cold water. Cook on stove for a half an hour, stirring occasionally until mixture is heated through and rice is soft.

Chicken cacciatore

I took an Italian cooking class not long ago with a good friend in the evenings at a local high school. It was a wonderful excuse to spend time together. Our instructor, a jovial, sixty year old, Lebanese man, peppered us with stories and jokes while his hands never stopped moving, chopping, kneading, stirring, tasting. Preparing food took the energy of his whole body and the results were delicious.

2 cups flour
½ tsp salt
¼ tsp black pepper
4 lbs boneless chicken breast, thighs or legs
2 tbsp olive oil
1 onion, chopped
3 cloves garlic, minced
1 green bell pepper, chopped
1 (14 oz) can diced tomatoes
½ tsp dried oregano
½ cup white wine
Dash of hot sauce
2 cups fresh mushrooms, quartered
Salt and pepper to taste

Combine flour, salt and pepper in a plastic bag. Shake the chicken pieces in flour until coated. Heat the oil in a large skillet with a lid. Fry the chicken pieces until they are browned on all sides. Remove from pan and set aside.

Add the onion, garlic and bell pepper to the pan and fry until onion is slightly browned. Return chicken to the pan and add tomatoes, oregano, wine and hot sauce. Cover and simmer for 30 minutes over low medium heat.

Add the mushrooms and salt and pepper to taste. Simmer for 10 minutes longer.

Grilled and glazed salmon

Going steady is a chance to dream together, to picture your lives together. This dish, when I first prepared it, caused me to reflect on the two of us; how a simple, healthful salmon covered in a many-flavoured, complex sauce, at once salty and sweet, becomes something greater when paired, that salty tears and sweet moments will often mingle and compete in our lives, but mixed, gives our life its texture.

2 cloves garlic, minced
2 tbsp olive oil
1 tbsp grated fresh ginger
½ cup orange juice
¼ cup hoisin sauce
¼ cup Madeira or dark rum
2 tbsp soy sauce
1 med orange cut into thin slices, each slice cut in half
4 to 6 Pacific salmon steaks or fillets

Cook garlic in oil in a small saucepan over medium heat until softened, about 2 minutes. Stir in the remaining ingredients except the salmon and bring to a boil. Simmer the sauce about 15 minutes or slightly thickened. Place salmon on squares of aluminum foil.

Grill over medium-high heat with the cover down about 10 minutes.

Brush with the glaze and continue to cook 2 to 3 minutes longer or until the fish is cooked. Serve fish with additional warm sauce spooned over each portion.

Grilled trout with tomato salsa

Going steady is having your life companion, a partner to walk with, a friend to laugh with, a shoulder to cry upon, a lover to cherish, another who knows your heart. Many of my recipes, including this one, include a pairing, a main ingredient and an accompaniment. It is no coincidence that the best results come from coupling. Prepare both and savour the taste of oneness.

2 firm, field tomatoes, diced
1 cup cucumber, diced
¼ cup fresh basil, chopped
2 tsp red wine vinegar or lime juice
2 cloves garlic, minced
1 lbs fresh trout fillets, rinsed
2 tbsp canola oil
Salt and pepper to taste

In a large bowl, gently combine tomatoes, cucumber, basil, vinegar and garlic. Set aside.

Brush trout lightly with oil on both sides and sprinkle with salt and pepper to taste. Place trout skin side down on greased grill over high heat. Reduce heat to medium, close lid and grill about five to ten minutes, depending on thickness or until fish is opaque and flakes easily. Remove with a long metal spatula and serve immediately with tomato salsa spooned over top.

Baked whole salmon with white wine sauce

I love to prepare this dish in the spring, when the world is coming alive, all green shoots and colourful flowers. Serve a noble salmon thus prepared with steamed fresh asparagus or tender fiddleheads and baby new potatoes to greet the promise of spring.

7 to 10 lb whole salmon
¾ wine
¼ tsp thyme
½ tsp basil
¼ tsp tarragon
¼ tsp crushed rosemary
celery leaves
3 shallots, minced
2 slices lemon peel

Preheat oven to 375F degrees.

Rinse salmon and pat dry. Put wine in saucepan and add remaining ingredients. Simmer uncovered a half an hour. Do not boil. Lay fish in foil and fold edges at side. Pour in wine mixture. Close foil completely. Bake for 2 hours or until flakes with fork. Serve with white wine sauce.

White Wine Sauce

½ cup butter
2 shallots finely chopped
6 tbsp flour
liquid in which salmon was baked
equal parts of dry white wine and boiling water
½ cup heavy cream
salt and pepper to taste
2 eggs yolks
dash hot sauce

Melt butter and fry shallots until transparent. Using wire whisk beat in flour until well blended. Cook over low heat for 3 minutes. Let stand until fish is cooked. When fish is cooked add juices to flour mixture stirring constantly over moderate heat. Stir vigorously while adding wine to make cups.

Ecuadorian ceviche

This is a funny, little recipe. I learned to prepare it one summer and was amazed at how much I enjoyed it. It was skeptical at first, despite the fact that it is enjoyed by nations of people, that it would please my palate. But it is pretty on your plate and beautiful on your tongue. It is a refreshing dish on an especially sultry, hot afternoon.

3 lbs cooked medium shrimp
1 large red onion, sliced thinly
6 limes, juiced
2 chopped tomatoes
4 tbsp white vinegar
¾ tsp black pepper
¾ tsp salt
2 tsp parsley, chopped
2 red or yellow peppers, sliced thinly

Pour boiling water over the red sliced onions, add some salt and pepper and let it stand for 15 minutes. Remove onions and wash in cold water.

Place cooked shrimp in a bowl and pour the lime juice over the shrimp. Add a pinch of salt and pepper. Let it stand for 15 minutes. Add remaining ingredients to the bowl and mix well. Allow shrimp to marinate in the refrigerator for one hour before serving.

Trout in orange juice

I spent two summers learning to fly fish. Certainly not a sport I ever thought I would learn or that would suit my temperament, I discovered to my pleasure that the sounds of running water, sunlight dancing on the ripples, the occasional call of a song bird and the rhythmic whooshing of the fly in the air was deeply satisfying. Besides, I learned to place my bait just so to nab my prey – useful in the dating arena. This recipe combines the fruits of those labours with my love of citrus.

4 rainbow trout fillets, cleaned and dried
2 tbsp pimento, diced
salt and pepper to taste
2 tbsp capers, drained and chopped
¼ cup lime juice
2 tbsp dry sherry
4 tbsp olive oil
½ cup orange juice
2 green onions, minced
1 clove garlic, crushed
1 large, very ripe tomato, peeled, seeded, chopped

Preheat oven to 350F degrees.

Put trout in shallow dish, sprinkle with salt, pepper and lime juice on both sides and let stand for 15 minutes. Grease a shallow baking dish with some oil, place fish on top, combine onions, garlic, tomato, pimento and capers an spread the mixture on top of the trout fillets. Sprinkle with remaining oil and bake in oven for 10 minutes. Pour orange juice and sherry over fish and bake another 10 to 15 minutes or until trout is done.

One summer during university, I took a summer job at a private, fishing club in the country. Built in the early 1900s, it was a large, four storey lodge, complete with massive stone fireplaces and a wrap around veranda overlooking the gardens, lawns and ponds on the property. The men who joined the club fished for rainbow, brown and brook trout in the stocked ponds and I worked in the lodge serving wine at meals and cleaning the fish caught that day. It was an idyllic oasis from another time, not much in touch with modernity or the rapid pace of day to day life, but rather an escape from life, a chance to slow down and step back. Even for us staff, we lived on site, either in the rafters of the main lodge, small, squeaky rooms hidden on the upper floor accessed through a back servant's staircase or in Goldie Lodge, a whitewashed, green-trimmed lodge above a garage, hidden among trees, walking distance from the lodge past a fish pond, bedrooms running off a main hallway, with a kitchen and sitting area. To be honest, it was a wonderful summer job, a chance to get to know new friends, enjoy nights sitting in that living room talking, laughing, complaining about guests, never realizing entirely what a unique and unrepeatable experience we were having.

I learned a lot about fish that summer. How to clean one, prepare and fillet a trout. I watched the chef prepare them, quickly, lightly, to preserve the fresh flaky taste of the freshly caught fish on the plate. I learned how to mix a brine to smoke the trout. I learned to gauge how many apple wood pucks to put in the smoker to give the flesh a particular taste, how much brown sugar to add to the brine, when to increase the spices when the fish were muddy in the mid-summer heat.

I learned that pansies taste peppery when added to a summer salad, that flakes of gold on Scotch broth make the serving more elegant, that being able to make a brown sauce is just as important as being able to make a white one. I watched the chef that summer and learned. I watched how wholesome food, when served with flair, becomes gourmet. I learned that sandwiches, a plate of cookies, a bowl of homemade soup and a pot of tea served on a veranda in the July sun is a repast. I tasted food I have never had, wild boar sausage, pickled tongue sandwiches, veal chop. I feel in love with variety but also with the pace with which the food was served. Meals always began with cocktails in the lounges or on the veranda. Wine accompanied dinner. Starters were savoured, mains enjoyed and dessert something to insist upon having.

I suppose I was younger but we rarely felt tired; we certainly worked hard and special events at the club were even larger undertakings and more work for us. But there was a tranquility about the club, a dream like quality that took us somewhere else, where time slowed, conversation was encouraged, silence was treasured, the swish of the fly in the air over the still pond something upon which to be mediated and meals, good food, good wine, something to respected, something for which it was important to slow down. Even now, I always insist that my guy and I sit down at the table for our meals, even when it is lowly soup or Kraft dinner or sandwiches. I take it from my mother's table. She insisted we eat together. Working at the trout club, this notion was reinforced. We staff became friends because we ate together. The club members and their guests became closer as they ate together. More and more, as I work on this cookbook and think about my experiences with food, I am realizing that the centre act of cooking and preparing food is to create community, communities in families, among friends and strangers, in private homes and in restaurants. In the pace of my current life, it is in sharing a meal perhaps the one moment when I consciously make time to connect.

Trout in the garden

This presentation is an unconventional way to prepare trout. The spinach, however, helps to retain the moisture in the flesh and, combined, the entire dish is a lovely casserole. Be certain to serve hot and enjoy immediately and do not be surprised if he reaches for more.

1 10 oz bags of fresh baby spinach
1 cup sour cream
¼ cup milk
3 tbsp flour
pinch of nutmeg
¼ tsp dill weed
1 small onion, minced
2 tbsp lemon juice
2 lbs rainbow trout fillets
2 tbsp butter
paprika

Preheat oven to 375F degrees.

Butter a 13 by 9 inch baking dish. Steam spinach and drain well. Blend sour cream, milk, flour, nutmeg, dill, onion, lemon juice and salt and pepper to taste. Mix half of this mixture with the spinach and spread in bottom of prepared pan. Lay fillets on top of spinach, dot fish with butter and spread with remaining sour cream mixture. Sprinkle with paprika. Bake about 25 minutes until fish is cooked. Serve immediately.

Savoury pork stew

This stew was a favourite autumn dish, redolent with the sharp bite of fresh apple cider, dark beer, mustard, cinnamon and dried fruit – it just feels warm and nourishing even in the reading. Serve on a chilly late autumn evening, with crusty bread and floury potatoes and finish with a fruit cobbler or crisp.

4 lbs pork should, trimmed and cubed
3 tbsp olive oil
2 large sliced onions
3 cloves minced garlic
¼ cup flour
2 cups chicken stock
1 cup apple cider or juice
1 ½ cup dark beer
1 tbsp Dijon mustard
1 tsp ground coriander
1 tsp cinnamon
1 cup chopped dried apricots
½ chopped prunes
salt and pepper

Preheat oven to 350F degrees.

Heat oil, add pork in batches, cook until brown, and transfer to a bowl.

Add onions and garlic to the pan and cook. Stir in flour and stir for three minutes. Mix in broth, cider, beer, mustard, coriander and cinnamon and bring to a boil.

Return pork and any juices to the pan. Stir in dried fruit. Cover and bake for one hour at 350F degrees.

Remove lid and continue baking for another 45 minutes or until pork is tender and liquid has sauce consistency. Season to taste and serve.

For some reason today, I am thinking about Christmas concerts as a child. I suppose it is probably because on Sunday we are going to a Christmas concert downtown with my parents. But today I am thinking of those simpler ones we use to do, with friends from class or Sunday school, all knees and elbows and piping voices, sweaty palms getting on stages and grins with gaps where teeth should be.

When I was small I remember going to Sunday school every Sunday. In what perhaps was a foreshadowing of my crazy need to be on time, I remember getting perfect attendance at Sunday school for five years running! Imagine what I was like as a child! I remember the worn linoleum floors of the Sunday school hall, the rubbed metal of the tracks which ran around the ceiling and from which hung faded rose-coloured curtains which could be pulled to create separate "classrooms" for teaching. I remember a great friend, Carolyn, in my class led by Mrs Dorington. Carolyn was learning to play the accordion. Can you imagine how marvelous that was and is, particularly now looking back, that this slight, little girl with bangs and braces was learning to play an accordion almost half the size she was? I remember being fascinated by it and even then not seeing anything peculiar or laugh-inducing in the fact that she was learning it only that she could manipulate bellows and keys and pegs all at the same time with her little stubby fingers. I remember the endless rehearsals for the Christmas concert and then performance night, families coming in from the snow, sitting in rows steaming with coats and gloves and mittens strung by a string through the sleeves of your coat from one side to the other. And the singing, loud, clear, off key likely, looking out at the church, warmed by the kid next to you, itchy in new wool pants, thinking about the desserts to be served downstairs afterward.

I still marvel that all those women provided so much food for so many occasions. I am not sure if you ever experienced a church supper or a church social but if nothing else it was always served up, the entire event, on long folding tables, covered in paper tablecloths, tapped underneath with masking tape. To this day I associate particular foods with church suppers, salmon sandwiches cut in triangles, jellied moulds, coffee served in enormous silver cylinders with spouts at the end like a pool with a drain, pickles in glass trays, devilled eggs with slashes of paprika strewn across the tops. At church suppers, the women would have prepared vast mounds of roast turkey on platters, mashed potatoes, peas and carrots, coleslaw made by the vat, pickles and pickled beets. And each woman would have baked a pie of varying fruits and styles. They would all be cut up, placed on mismatched crockery plates, loaded as an assortment on large plastic trays and then delivered to the tables so you could select your own finale to end the meal. Sticky mints, occasionally covered in lint, in glass bowls, bowls of clementines and trays of sugar cookies with coloured sprinkles, homemade butter tarts, and squares of every kind. It really was food in abundance, food for celebrating and rejoicing.

Grilled Dijon pork chops

When I was a child, pork chops were my absolute favourite. Grilled, fried, barbequed, they always set my mouth to watering. There was no greater treat for me than coming in from school to find my mother frying pork chops in her electric frying pan or deep, silver skillet on the stove, turning them when browned with a kitchen fork, the smell of garlic frying. I was always the first to reach for one sitting down at the table. This recipe adds the delicious richness of Dijon mustard to a classic.

4 thick pork chops
¼ cup Dijon mustard
3 tbsp teriyaki sauce
1 tsp olive oil
1 clove garlic, minced
1 tbsp fresh rosemary, chopped

Season pork chops with salt and pepper. Whisk together Dijon mustard, teriyaki sauce, olive oil, garlic and rosemary. Put chops in a sealable bad and pour in marinade. Coat chops and marinate for 5 to 20 minutes. Grill chops for approximately 4 minutes per side or until done.

So last night, I went with my dear friends Maryann and Julia out for dinner. Just the three of us, just to catch up. We had a marvelous time, as we always do, laughing, talking. We had a good meal and suddenly the evening was over. And here is my question: when did a bowl of spicy Shanghai noodles with crisp vegetables and a delicious glass (admittedly an oversized one) of deep red Sangiovese wine suddenly cost 35 bucks, 40 with a tip? Seriously, I remember when 40 dollars was my grocery bill for the week. Don't laugh we all remember those days, the days where cheap pork steaks riddled with fat, after being marinated in soy sauce and cooked in garlic, were a gourmet treat, where we had fifty different ways to prepare Kraft dinner, where soup could be stretched by constantly adding water to the kettle! All kidding aside, I remember running out of money at the end of the semester at university and eating peanut butter and jam sandwiches for lunch and for dinner for a month till school ended.

But you know, I imagine every family has a story of a crazy recipe that your mother served that somehow became a family favourite. In our case, it was something my mother called snorkel casserole. I have no idea where the name came from except maybe she dreamt it up while looking down at hungry faces standing in the kitchen fresh in from playing outside. I asked my mother once about it and she remembers it clearly. There was absolutely nothing in the cupboards to make for dinner and three days till payday and there she was faced with two young children and my father to feed that evening. So with the creativity of all mothers, she rummaged through the cupboards and threw together a casserole. And what a crazy combination it was: a couple of sliced onions on the bottom of the disk, some frozen peas tossed in, a couple of potatoes sliced and put in the pan, a handful of white rice and strangely a can of Campbell's vegetable soup and a half a can of water poured over it all. Mom fried some breakfast sausages found at the back of the freezer and laid them in rows over the top and baked it all for an hour. When we pulled up our chairs for dinner, my mother announced that tonight for dinner we were having snorkel casserole so dive in. And you know what it was really tasty; it quickly became my brother's favourite dinner and even now he will make it as an adult for himself, long after my mother stopped. I always laugh at that dish, but I know every family has a similar story, a story of bare cupboards and your mother's ingenuity and a new family favourite is born. Feeding your guy on a dime and prayer. Last night I laughed to think how fortunate I am right now that I can toss down two twenty dollar bills for nothing more than a bowl of noodles and fermented grapes. Times have changed but I know the day will come when my cupboards are looking equally bare and payday is a few days away and I pray that I will be as committed, ingenious and resourceful as my mother and that I can do it as cheerfully as she did, smiling, as she put snorkel casserole down on the kitchen table.

Snorkel casserole

What is there to say about this recipe, a family classic from my mother's creativity, my brother's favourite, an economical meal, a happy memory for me? Try it and see if you like it – imagine your own creations and bring them to your own table.

2 tbsp vegetable oil
1 package fast fry breakfast sausages
2 large potatoes, peeled and sliced thinly
½ cup long grain rice
½ cup frozen green peas
3 medium onions, sliced thinly
1 can Campbell's vegetable soup
½ cup water
salt and pepper to taste

Preheat oven to 350F degrees.

In a large glass baking dish, layer the potatoes and onions on the bottom. Season with salt and pepper. Add rice and peas, spreading evenly over bottom. In a small bowl, mix soup concentrate and water and pour over casserole. Set aside.

In a skillet, heat oil over medium heat. Add sausages and fry, turning regularly, until sausages are cooked and golden brown. Remove from pan, drain on absorbent paper to remove excess fat.

Lay the cooked sausages in a single layer over the casserole mixture. Bake in the oven for 1 hour or until potatoes are tender.

Roast pork tenderloin with apricot glaze

I think people have forgotten pork in today's chicken dominated cuisine. Pork, when well prepared, is moist, succulent and deeply satisfying. It is among my father's favourites and is always a welcome change from weeknight chicken. This dish is large enough that it feeds tonight, provides leftovers tomorrow, and a delicious sandwich in your guy's lunch on the third day.

1 ½ lbs pork tenderloin
2 tbsp water
¼ tsp fresh rosemary, chopped
¼ cup apricot jam
1 tbsp brandy
2 tbsp olive oil
1 clove garlic, crushed
coarse salt and pepper to taste

Preheat oven to 350F degrees.

In a glass bowl, combine water, rosemary, apricot jam, brandy, olive oil, crushed garlic and coarse salt and pepper and mix well until blended. Place pork in glaze and cover its surface thoroughly.

Place pork on a rack in an open roasting pan. All roast to cook for about 40 minutes or until meat is tender. Turn over and brush with glaze while roasting. Once cooked to your preference, remove from oven and allow to rest before serving. Serve with apricots.

Baked macaroni and cheese

Who does not love macaroni and cheese? If you have only ever had the instant boxed or frozen version of this timeless classic, you have been missing out, almost like assuming a wave pool really feels like the tides of the sea. The difference is monumental. This dish is a perfect lazy, rainy afternoon dish – once tried, you will never date another.

4 cups elbow macaroni
1 tbsp butter
3 tbsp flour
1 tbsp dry mustard
3 cups milk
½ cup yellow onion, diced finely
½ tsp paprika
1 bay leaf
1 large egg
1 ½ cups sharp cheddar, shredded
Fresh black pepper

Topping:

3 tbsp butter
1 cup dry bread crumbs

In a large pot of boiling, salted water cook the pasta al dente.

While pasta is cooking, in a separate pot, melt the butter. Whisk in flour and mustard and stir continuously for five minutes. Do not allow mixture to clump. Stir in milk, onion, bay leaf and paprika. Simmer for ten minutes and remove the bay leaf.

Add egg to hot mixture slowly. Stir in ¾ of the cheese. Season with salt and pepper. Fold in the macaroni into the mixture and pour into a 2 quart casserole dish. Top with remaining cheese.

Melt butter in a saucepan and toss the breadcrumbs to coat. Sprinkle casserole with bread crumbs. Bake for 30 minutes. Remove from oven and let rest for 5 minutes prior to serving.

So here it is, lunch hour, and I am sitting at my desk, day dreaming about Greece. It wasn't long ago that my guy and I were in the shade of an ancient olive tree, happily slurping on our ice cream treats. From our vantage point, I could look up at the Acropolis where we had just spent the last three hours.

I studied classical civilization as my major at university and to have the chance to visit the Acropolis and see and touch the Parthenon was truly amazing to me. To imagine the effort, intellect and determination that was required to build that perfect edifice and to keep a group of people focused for forty years on its construction spoke to me of our capacity to create, to dream and to make our dreams reality. It is a testament to what we can achieve when we set our minds to it. Awesome. Inspiring. Motivating. I have friends who have done the Ironman Marathon or cycle for charity, who paint or sing or dance, who build with their hands or minds: so many friends who in their own ways have found their inspiration and chased it.

And sitting there, in that sun-dappled shade, eating my ice cream and looking at the Parthenon, I was reminded to keep chasing my dream. But only for an instant, because honestly, I was caught in the spell of Greece, the olives turning purple above me, the light on the stones, the absolute blue sky framing the temple, the warm sun, the cool breeze and my lover at my side. It wasn't long before we got up, ambled down the road, and eventually found a sticky, sweet piece of baklava to share. Sometimes life is not for thinking, not for planning. Sometimes life is just for living.

Pumpkin ravioli

My guy has an endless fount of patience. I barely have enough to fill a thimble. He is patient with my foibles, my endless planning, my foul moods, my weaknesses. He is also patient in teasing out my potential, my dreams, my secret hopes and desires. I have learned to appreciate his patience and not too frequently to abuse it. Patience can be mysterious and life giving. Have patience in making this recipe – the effort is well spent.

1 cup pumpkin puree
1 tbsp butter, cut into tiny pieces
1 ½ tsp cornmeal
1 tsp dried sage, crumbled
½ tsp dried thyme
Salt and pepper to taste
36 wonton wrappers
1 egg, beaten
¼ cup butter, melted

In a medium bowl, combine pumpkin puree, cut butter, cornmeal, sage, thyme, salt and pepper to taste. Working with six wrappers at a time, brush edges lightly with beaten egg. Place one heaping teaspoon of pumpkin mixture in the centre of each wrapper. Fold each wrapper over into a triangle and press the edges to seal well. Place on a baking sheet and cover with a damp towel. Repeat with remaining wrappers and filling.

In a large pot of boiling water, cook the ravioli in four batches until tender, about four to five minutes per batch. Remove with a slotted spoon. Gently toss with melted butter and serve immediately with a sprinkling of Parmesan cheese and a dash of nutmeg.

Roasted butternut squash lasagna

This example of lasagna is a new twist on the classic meat version. At first, you may think it strange to imagine lasagna with squash but this dish dances magnificently on your tongue, blending its tastes into something altogether new. Sure to become a favourite.

2 lbs butternut squash, peeled
1 large sweet onion, chopped
¼ cup butter, melted
1 tbsp honey
2 cloves garlic, minced
1 tbsp fresh rosemary leaves, chopped
½ tsp each salt and pepper
4 cups cottage cheese
¾ cup each milk and low sodium vegetable broth
1 ¼ cups Gorgonzola cheese, crumbled
9 oz fresh lasagna noodles, about six
1 ½ cup fresh breadcrumbs
½ cup chopped walnuts
¼ fresh parsley leaves, chopped

Preheat oven to 450F degrees. Cut squash into small cubes. Toss the squash and onion with half the melted butter, honey, garlic, rosemary, salt and pepper until well combined. Spread in a single layer on a parchment lined baking sheet. Roast, turning occasionally, for 20 to 25 minutes or until very tender. Cool slightly then combine with cottage cheese, milk, broth and Gorgonzola cheese.

Reduce the oven to 350F degrees. Grease a 9 by 13 inch baking dish. Spread one quarter of the cottage cheese mixture evenly into the dish. Cover with an even layer of noodles, trimming to fit. Repeat layers of cheese and noodles twice. Spread the remaining cheese mixture evenly over the noodles.

Cover with foil and bake for 45 minutes. Remove foil and bake uncovered for 15 minutes. Meanwhile, toss breadcrumbs with walnuts, parsley and remaining melted butter. Sprinkle the lasagna evenly with breadcrumb mixture. Broil for three minutes or until browned. Rest for twenty minutes before slicing.

Spicy chickpea stew

This is a wonderfully simple stew that has become a winner with my guy. I am always looking for new recipes to include more vegetables into our diet and this stew is spicy, satisfying and makes a filling dinner. Serve alone or heaped over hot steamed rice.

2 (19 oz) can cooked chickpeas, rinsed and drained
5 cups vegetable broth
3 large potatoes, peeled and diced
3 large tomatoes, diced
2 tsp garam masala
½ tsp ground ginger
½ tsp ground tumeric
salt and pepper to taste
chopped coriander to garnish

In a large saucepan or skillet with lid, add broth, chickpeas, tomatoes, potatoes, garam masala, ginger and turmeric. Bring to a boil, reduce heat, cover and simmer until potatoes are tender, about 30 minutes.

Remove from heat and let cool slightly. Transfer 3 cups of broth and vegetables to a food processor and blend until smooth. Return to saucepan and season with salt and pepper. Reheat to serving temperature. Serve into warmed bowls, sprinkle with coriander. Serve hot.

Easy cheesy casserole

If you have children, nieces or nephews or even random neighbourhood children nearby, this casserole is a huge hit with the under ten crowd. It is easy to prepare, easy to serve and only one skillet to wash. One tip: when you heat salsa, it becomes spicier. For milder casserole, use mild salsa, for fiery casserole, use hot salsa. Prepare extra, the kids will ask for more.

1 lb ground beef, chicken or turkey
1 can Campbells' Cheddar soup
1 cup medium salsa
3 green onions, diced
2 cups cooked pasta, shells, swirls or macaroni
1 cup shredded old cheddar

Brown the meat in a deep saucepan until well cooked, seasoning to taste. Add the can of soup, salsa and onions and cook together for 3 minutes. Add drained cooked pasta and combine, cook for 2 minutes, mixing well. Add shredded cheese and cook until cheese is melted through and mixture is hot. Serve immediately.

Wild mushroom risotto

I make this recipe just for me. Above all else, this recipe teaches me patience and the rewards of taking my time. I love watching the risotto develop under my care and am always delighted when suddenly it is ready.

½ cup dried porcini or morel mushrooms
5 cups vegetable stock
1 lb mixed fresh wild mushrooms, halved
4 tbsp olive oil
4 cloves garlic, minced
1 onion, finely chopped
1 ¾ cup Arborio rice
¼ cup dry white vermouth
1 cup freshly grated Parmesan cheese
4 tbsp chopped fresh flat leaf parsley
salt and pepper to taste

Place the dried mushrooms in a heatproof bowl and add boiling water to cover. Set aside to soak for 30 minutes then lift out and dry. Strain liquid through a strainer lined with paper towels and set aside.

Bring the stock to a boil in a pan, then reduce heat and keep simmering gently over low heat while you are cooking the rice. Trim and clean the fresh mushrooms. Heat 3 tbsp of oil in a skillet, add mushrooms and cook for 2 minutes, add garlic and soaked mushrooms and cook for 2 minutes longer. Remove from heat

Heat the remaining oil and butter in a large deep heavy bottom pan. Add the onion and cook stirring occasionally until softened. Reduce the heat and add the rice to the butter and oil and cook for 2-3 minutes until rice is translucent. Add the vermouth and cook, stirring constantly, for 1 minute until reduced.

Gradually add the stock one ladle full at a time. Stir constantly and add more broth as it is absorbed. Increase the heat to medium so the liquid bubbles and cook for 20 minutes or until the rice is creamy. Add half the reserved mushroom liquid to the risotto and stir in the mushrooms. Season with salt and pepper to taste and add more mushroom liquid as required. Remove from heat and stir in remaining butter, grated Parmesan and chopped parsley. Serve at once.

Saffron and lemon risotto with scallops

This is the perfect risotto to prepare when you want to impress, especially a potential mother-in-law. It requires patience in making the risotto, care and timing when searing the scallops and presents beautifully. This dish is decadent when thoughtfully prepared but appears simple and carefree, perfect for making the suggestion that you simply threw this together in a hurry just before her arrival.

16 fresh scallops, shucked
juice of one lemon
5 cups vegetable stock
1 tbsp olive oil
3 tbsp butter
1 small onion, finely chopped
1 ½ cups Arborio rice
1 tsp crumbled saffron threads
2 tbsp olive oil
1 cup freshly grated Parmesan cheese
salt and pepper to taste

Place the scallops in a nonmetallic bowl and mix with the lemon juice. Cover the bowl with plastic wrap and let chill in the refrigerator for 15 minutes.

Bring the stock to a boil in a bake and then reduce heat and keep simmering. Heat the oil with 2 tbsp of butter in a deep pan over medium heat, add the onion and cook, stirring occasionally, for 5 minutes or until soft. Add the rice and coat in oil and butter. Cook, stirring, for 2-3 minutes or until grains are translucent. Dissolve the saffron in 4 tbsp of stock and add to the rice. Gradually add the remaining stock, a ladleful at a time, as it is absorbed and until rice is creamy. Season to taste.

When risotto is nearly cooked, preheat a grill pan. Brush scallops with oil and sear on pan for 3-4 minutes on each side. Remove risotto from heat, add remaining butter, mix well, then stir in Parmesan cheese. Season with lemon juice to taste.

Place a large scoop of risotto on each plate, top with four scallops and garnish with lemon wedges and lemon zest, serve at once.

Hot pepper lamb in red wine risotto

A man's risotto, this one. Succulent, rich lamb is paired with creamy risotto, married together by a deep, wine infused sauce. This risotto will satisfy his desire for a hearty meal while bringing a touch of elegance to your table.

4 tbsp flour
8 pieces of lamb or lamb chops
4 tbsp olive oil
1 green bell pepper, cleaned and thinly sliced
2 small onions, 1 thinly sliced, 1 finely chopped
2 close garlic, thinly sliced
2 tbsp torn fresh basil
½ cup red wine
4 tbsp red wine vinegar
8 cherry tomatoes
½ cup water
5 cups chicken stock
3 tbsp butter
1 ½ cups Arborio rice
¾ cup freshly grated Parmesan cheese
salt and pepper to taste

Mix flour, salt and pepper on a plate. Coat lamb in flour and brown in hot oil in a large ovenproof casserole until brown on all sides. Set aside. Toss the pepper, sliced onion, garlic, and basil in oil left in casserole until lightly browned. Add the wine and vinegar, bring to a boil and continue cooking for 3-4 minutes or until liquid is reduce. Add the tomatoes and water, stir and bring to a boil. Return meat to the casserole, cover, reduce heat to low. Cook for 30 minutes or until meat is tender, turning occasionally. Add water if necessary.

Bring stock to a boil in a pot, reduce to low and keep simmering. Heat remaining oil with 2 tbsp of butter, add chopped onion and cook stirring occasionally for 5 minutes or until onion is soft. Reduce heat, add rice to oil and butter and cook for 2-3 minutes or until rice is translucent. Gradually add hot stock, one ladleful at a time, stirring constantly, adding more stock as rice absorbs all the liquid. Increase heat to medium so mixture bubbles, cook for 20 minutes longer or until rice is creamy.

Remove risotto from heat and add remaining butter, mix well and add Parmesan until melted. Arrange a scoop of risotto on each plate and top with peppers and tomatoes. Top all with lamb and serve.

Black bean stew with spinach

This stew is exceptionally nourishing. Packed with beans and spinach, it is high in fibre, protein and iron, ginger adds a boost to the immune system, tomatoes aid in the fight against free radicals and may prevent cancer, garlic cleanses the blood and aids in lowering cholesterol, olive oil gives us essential fats and onions clear the skin. This stew is a delicious, health promoting superhero.

1 tbsp olive oil
1 onion, chopped
3 cloves garlic, minced
1 tbsp mild curry paste
2 tsp fresh ginger, minced
Salt and pepper to taste
1 can (28 oz) diced tomatoes
1 can (19 oz) black beans, washed and drained
4 cup packed fresh baby spinach

In a Dutch oven, heat oil over medium heat. Fry onion, garlic, curry paste, salt and pepper until onion is softened, about 3 minutes. Add tomatoes and beans, bring to a boil. Reduce heat and simmer until thickened, about 15 minutes. Stir in spinach, heat until wilted, about 2 minutes.

Falafel

I love falafel. I learned how to make this easy to prepare home cooked version in an evening cooking class at the local high school. These falafel are spicy, savoury and hearty and are delicious served traditionally in a pita with lettuce, parsley, onions, tomatoes and garlic sauce or equally atop a fresh garden salad for lunch.

1 cup canned chickpeas, drained
½ cup canned fava beans, drained
1 large onion, diced
1 large potato, quartered
½ bunch flat leaf parsley, washed
¼ bunch coriander, washed
4 cloves garlic
1 tsp cumin
½ tsp cayenne pepper
1 tsp salt
3 tbsp sesame seeds
1 pinch baking soda
Oil for frying

Process all ingredients except sesame seeds, baking soda and oil in a food processor until a medium fine paste is formed. Add sesame seeds and soda and mix well.

Form small balls with your hands and deep fry in hot oil until golden brown. Serve in pitas or with fresh salad, radishes, pickles and onions.

One glorious afternoon, we wandered slowly through the souk and ancient Jewish market in the Old City of Jerusalem. Passing through the Jaffa gate was like stepping back into a forgotten time: narrow, cobblestone streets worn smooth by the endless feet of pilgrims from three faiths journeying through the city, loud vendors calling their wares, dust, donkey dung, incense hanging in the air, flowers blooming riotously on the old walls. We trod slowly through the souk, the bright autumn sun almost completely shut out by the stalls of merchants selling everything from radios to leather goods, from bras to sweets. I was assaulted by the smells from the spice merchant, cardamom, cinnamon, peppers, nutmegs, cumin, coriander, herbal teas, salad spices, each one filling my nose with promise. Bakeries with olive pizzas and manoush, flat breads covered with zatar, a spice mixture of oregano. I could pick my way through piles of dates, pistachios, dried nuts, apricots, figs, mangos, kiwis, sample halwa, sesame snacks with pistachios or fruit in them or leisurely choose loosely-piled candies of every sort. No plastic wrappers here: simply dig and select.

There is something about shopping in a market that has stood for thousands of years, and something else again to shop in the market, aware of the thousands of pilgrims, Crusaders, defenders, thieves, adventurers, poets and families that have come for evening dinner through the centuries. I fell in love with Jerusalem, with its three great faiths shouldered one against the other, its storied walls, narrow streets, surprising squares and history everywhere you turned. In a little shop, on a well-trodden side street, I stuck my pinkie finger into date honey and fell in love. Date honeys are also mixed with caramel or sesame and deliciously spread over toast in the morning with strong coffee. I felt as though I had stuck my pinkie finger into Jerusalem and got the most fleeting but sweet taste of the place.

We ate later that day at an Armenian restaurant, aptly located in the Armenian quarter. We nibbled on appetizers of sour cabbage, pickled carrots, potato salad, cucumbers, beautiful hummus and freshly baked pita breads. A cold local beer, a breeze from the backyard patio through the open window, the cool of the stone-vaulted roof overhead and lunch with new friends was underway. I understand completely now the ancient Jewish saying, next year, Jerusalem. I fell in love with the place. All my senses were afire there: the hue of the light, the multi-coloured goods in the souk, the call to prayer, the bells, the singing wailing wall in your ears, the feel of history underfoot, the texture of the walls, streets, water splashing over your hands in fountains, but more than all, the smells of spices, sweets, meats, bread, life in the air.

Mushroom cheddar cheese strudel

Pick a weekend and invite three of your favourite couples over to the house for cocktails. Run out and buy a crisp, white wine and a deeply drinkable red, and a case of lager. Clean the house, put out some candles for soft lighting, put some light jazz on, prepare some hors d'oeuvres and then make this strudel. Open the wine, enjoy your friends and take this strudel, golden brown and bubbling with cheese from the oven and serve hot to your guests.

1 tbsp butter
½ tsp salt
½ cup onion, diced
¼ tsp pepper
1 tsp garlic, minced
4 cups mushrooms, sliced
1 cup potato, cooked and diced
1 ¼ cup old cheddar cheese, grated
6 sheets phyllo pastry
Melted butter
1 egg whisked with water
Poppy seeds

Preheat oven to 350F degrees.

Melt butter in a sauce pan until foaming. Add mushrooms, onions, garlic and spices and cook until liquid from mushrooms has evaporated. Add diced potatoes and grated cheese. Stir until cheese is melted; remove from heat.

Layer sheets of phyllo pastry on each other brushing each layer with butter before layering. Spoon filling along long edge of pastry. Roll up pastry to cover filling and lift onto prepared baking sheet. Press ends of pastry to seal. Brush the strudel with egg wash and sprinkle with poppy seeds. Bake for 30 to 40 minutes or until golden. Let cool 10 minutes before slicing and serving.

Divine scalloped potatoes

Is there ever an evening when hot, creamy scalloped potatoes are not a great accompaniment to dinner? Scalloped potatoes always seemed to pop up in the most unexpected places in my life, in the arms of that seldom seen aunt coming to visit, on buffet tables in church basements, on friends' tables at after school impromptu invitations to dinner or paired with ham for Easter dinner. Enjoy them freshly made and doubly enjoy them as leftovers.

8-10 large potatoes, peeled and sliced thinly
3 medium onions, sliced thinly
1 cup mushrooms, cleaned and sliced
2 cups old cheddar cheese, shredded
½ cup butter, melted
¼ cup flour
2 cups milk
1 cup whipping cream
dash cayenne
salt and pepper to taste
1 cup breadcrumbs

Preheat oven to 325F degrees.

In a lightly greased large baking casserole dish, place a single layer of potatoes on bottom. Place a layer of mushrooms, onions and cheese. Season with salt and pepper. Continue layering in the same pattern, seasoning with salt and pepper at each layer until casserole is ¾ full.

In a separate bowl, whisk together butter, flour, milk, whipping cream and dash of cayenne. Pour mixture over potatoes layers, allowing milk mixture to fill casserole. Cover top of potato layers with breadcrumbs and additional shredded cheese if desired.

Bake in a slow oven for 2 hours or until potatoes are tender and bubbling.

Smashed potatoes

You can laugh outright or discretely smile behind your hand at me for including this recipe in the cookbook if you like. I can hear you asking me who exactly does not know how to prepare potatoes or how to mash them. Well, first these are smashed, subtle perhaps, but it adds to their enjoyment and for some reason completely unknown to me, smashed they retain their flavour better than mashed. Save your teasing and try them – I know you will love them.

16 baby potatoes
1/3 cup fresh basil, stems discarded, minced
6 cloves garlic, minced
¼ cup olive oil
½ tsp salt
½ tsp freshly ground black pepper

Preheat oven to 400F degrees. Roast potatoes, skin on, for approximately 30 minutes or until cook throughout and crispy on the outside.

In a large bowl, add garlic, basil, olive oil, salt and pepper. Add roasted potatoes. Us a fork or whisk to smash potatoes, but do not mash. Toss thoroughly so potatoes are coated with oil, herbs and spices.

Potato and cauliflower curry

I learned to prepare this curry in my Indian cooking class. Whenever I announce that I am making Indian for dinner, this dish is the first one my guy asks me to include. It has become a great favourite of his and, candidly, it is to easy to prepare it is impossible to deny him. My only advice is this; make sure the cauliflower and potato are cut small, they cook faster and keep some extra water aside to add if it begins to stick. Otherwise, prepare it and enjoy – it also freezes well.

1 large cauliflower, clean and cut in florets
4 large potatoes, peeled and cut in cubes
¼ cup oil
1 tsp cumin seed
2 medium tomatoes, chopped
3 cloves garlic, minced
2 inch piece of ginger, minced
1 tsp salt
1 tsp red chili powder
¾ tsp turmeric
1 tsp garam masala
2 tbsp coriander leaves, chopped
½ cup water

Heat oil in a skillet and cook cumin seed for a minutes. Add garlic and ginger, cook for a minutes. Add salt, turmeric and chili powder, stir well. Add tomatoes and cook for 5 minutes. Add potatoes and cauliflower and cook for 15 minutes or until both are soft. Add water as needed and stir frequently to prevent burning. Add garam masala and mix well. Garnish with chopped coriander leaves.

Garlic mashed potatoes with olive oil

I know I have told you already that I am a huge fan of the potato. This recipe is more evidence of my obsession. This recipe is low in fat, easy to prepare and has mellowed the taste of the garlic to a fine, creamy hint. Serve with any meal as you would with mashed potatoes. This recipe is especially good when served with Irish Guinness beef stew.

6 large baking potatoes, peeled and quartered
1 large bay leaf
12 large cloves garlic, peeled
¼ cup vegetable broth
2 tbsp olive oil
Salt and pepper to taste

Place the potatoes and bay leaf in a large saucepan with salted water to cover, bring to a boil. Add the garlic cloves and reduce heat to medium high. Cook for 20 minutes or until potatoes are very tender. Drain well.

Transfer mixture to a serving bowl; remove bay leaf. Mash with a potato masher or fork. Add the broth and oil and mash until the mixture is not quite smooth. Season with salt and pepper and serve hot.

Roasted potatoes with oregano and lemon

My obsession with potatoes continues. Honestly, sometimes I prepare these potatoes in the afternoon just as a snack. I would make them everyday if my guy would let me. Often, when he is away, I will prepare them and enjoy them in guilty silence, never owning up to the fact that I have devoured an entire pan of potatoes. Great with summer barbeques or, in my case, a late afternoon snack, they are always a treat.

2 lbs russet potatoes, peeled and quartered lengthwise
2 tbsp olive oil
2 tsp dried oregano
2 large cloves garlic, minced
Salt and pepper to taste
½ cup vegetable broth
½ cup water
3 tbsp lemon juice

Preheat oven to 450F degrees. Lightly oil a shallow baking dish. Add the potatoes in a single layer and drizzle with oil, tossing well to coat. Sprinkle with oregano, garlic, salt and pepper. Toss again.

Combine broth, water and lemon juice. Pour evenly over potatoes. Roast uncovered for 1 hour, turning frequently with a spatula, until potatoes are tender and golden brown. Serve warm.

Lemon herb rice

I learned to make this recipe from my friend Soula, this rice reflecting her Mediterranean origins as clearly as her olive complexion and easy laugh. The lemon peel and juice add a stronger than expected flavour to this simple dish. Serve with barbequed chicken and lemon wedges for a tangy meal or with any fish or vegetables.

1 ½ tbsp olive oil
2 tbsp onion, finely chopped
1 cup long grain rice
2 cups vegetable broth
2 tbsp fresh lemon juice
½ tsp lemon zest, freshly grated
¼ tsp dried thyme
Salt and pepper to taste
2 tbsp fresh basil or mint, finely chopped

In a medium saucepan, heat oil over medium low heat. Add onion and cook for 3 minutes or until translucent. Add rice and increase heat to medium; cook, stirring for 1 minute. Add broth, lemon juice, lemon peel, thyme, salt and pepper. Bring to a boil, reduce heat and simmer until liquid is absorbed and rice is creamy, about 17 to 20 minutes. Add fresh herbs, combine, let stand 1 minute, fluff and serve.

Asparagus in orange sauce

In Spain, the last harvest of winter oranges are paired with the first tender shoots of spring asparagus in this fresh light preparation of this classic vegetable. Together, they pair to present a delicate and sophisticated taste on the palate which can grace an elegant affair or a weeknight meal.

1 ½ lbs asparagus, ends trimmed
½ cup fresh orange juice
½ cup white wine
½ cup vegetable broth
½ tsp olive oil
Salt and pepper to taste

Bring a large pot of salted water to a boil, add asparagus and cook until just tender, about 3 to 4 minutes. Drain and refresh under running cold water, drain and return to pot.

In a small saucepan, bring orange juice, wine and broth to a boil. Reduce until ¼ cup remains. Whisk in oil. Pour over the asparagus, tossing well to coat, season with salt and pepper. Heat over low heat until asparagus are hot. Serve warm.

Baked cabbage with garlic

I will admit the first time I prepared cabbage in this fashion I was skeptical. The recipe seemed too simple. The cabbage could have been bland, the seasonings insufficient, the garlic repetitive. I prepared this dish, popped it in the oven and soon smelled, with great anticipation, the mingling of these flavours. My guy came to the kitchen and asked what was for dinner; soon I was ladling it onto his plate. His first sigh of pleasure told me I had hit the mark.

1 small firm cabbage, cored and quartered
1 ½ tbsp olive oil
2 cloves garlic, minced
¼ cup vegetable broth
Salt and pepper to taste

Preheat oven to 425F degrees. Lightly oil a deep baking dish.

Fill a saucepan deep enough to take a steaming basket with boiling water. Add cabbage to basket, lower into saucepan and steam carefully until softened, approximately 7 to 10 minutes. Remove and transfer to the baking dish. Set aside.

In a small saucepan, heat the oil, add garlic and cook for 2 minutes. Spoon garlic evenly over cabbage. Add broth to the dish and season with salt and pepper. Cover the dish tightly with lid or foil and bake for 20 minutes or until cabbage is tender. Serve hot with cooking liquid spooned over each portion.

Baked onions

A friend told me about these little, unheard of, half-whispered rounds of decadence. Do not underestimate or overlook this recipe. With baking, these onions become candy sweet, caramelizing while holding their shape. Serve beside roast beef, steak or enjoy on their own, if like me, onions are a favourite.

4 small yellow onions, peeled
6 tsp olive oil
Salt and pepper to taste
4 tsp unseasoned bread crumbs

Preheat oven to 350F degrees. Bring a large saucepan of water to a boil. Add onions, reduce heat slightly and simmer for 5 minutes. Drain and let cool slightly.

Cut onions in half crosswise. Lightly oil a baking dish just large enough to hold all the onions in a single layer. Rub onions with oil and place snugly in the baking dish. Season each with salt and pepper, sprinkle with ½ tsp of breadcrumb and drizzle oil over top of each half. Bake for 1 hour and 15 minutes or until tops are browned and caramelized. Serve warm.

Corsican baked tomatoes

Like baked onions, these baked tomatoes only intensity in flavour with the long, slow baking. Besides being absolutely delicious, the baked tomatoes are especially good for your guy's health, helping to prevent future prostate problems and providing concentrated vitamin C. Stop worrying just about their health giving properties and enjoy them alone or served over rice or hearty, Italian bread.

4 large tomatoes, cut in half
Salt and pepper to taste
1 cup fresh flat leaf parsley, finely chopped
2 large cloves garlic, minced
4 tbsp olive oil

Preheat oven to 450F degrees. Lightly oil a casserole or baking dish large enough to hold tomatoes halves snugly. Sprinkle tomatoes with salt and pepper. In a small bowl, combine parsley and garlic. Stuff each tomato with the parsley mixture, about 2 tablespoons per tomato.

Arrange tomatoes in baking dish snugly. Drizzle with olive oil. Bake for 20 minutes. Reduce heat to 350F degrees and bake 1 hour longer or until tomatoes are very tender and caramelized. Serve warm or at room temperature.

Caramelized roasted squash

I love squash. I always have. In fact, I love almost everything about squash. I enjoy planting those flat white seeds in the cool, moist spring earth and later feeling dirt under my nails as I mound the squash hill. I love how the water pools on its dark green leaves in the hot summer, the bright orange cone-shaped flowers peeking from below. I love watching them form and mature and after that first frost, finding themselves on my cutting board to be baked in this tantalizing recipe flavoured with real maple syrup.

¼ cup balsamic vinegar
¼ cup extra virgin olive oil
¼ cup maple syrup
1 butternut squash
1 red onion, peeled and cut into wedges
¼ tsp salt
¼ tsp black pepper
1 tbsp fresh thyme leaves

Preheat oven to 400F degrees. In a bowl, whisk together vinegar, oil, maple syrup, salt and pepper. Cut squash in half lengthwise. Scoop out seeds. Place the cut side down on the cutting board. Cut in half crosswise. Cut into wedges 1 inch or 2.5 cm thick at the peel. In a large bowl, toss squash and onion with the vinegar mixture. Place on a rimmed baking sheet. Bake in the centre of the oven for 30 minutes. Turn the vegetables and bake another 20 to 25 minutes or until squash is tender. Sprinkle with thyme.

Happy endings

We got married last year on a July afternoon in the back garden of a century-old stone manor house surround by our family and friends. My nieces and nephews ran around, my sister-in-law sang for us and the only ones with tears in their eyes were my guy and me.

Despite having planned the food so carefully, I did not taste a single hors d'oeuvre, only picked at my salad, barely remember my dinner, only setting aside my dessert to indulge my love of crème brulee after speeches. I completely missed the sweets table. My memories of that day are filled with smiling, laughing faces of the people I love, the feel of my husband's arms around me on the dance floor, the taste and texture of cake on my tongue, the pressure of my guy's hand in mine, and the knowledge that my hand will be held secure in his for many, many years to come.

Marriage, we are discovering, is a separate thing, sublime and mysterious, demanding and rewarding. It has changed us already and I am awed by the future that we can build together, one larger than each of us alone, one filled with gifts unknown, of tears comforted, laughter shared, happiness doubled, troubles eased, challenges faced.

There is a certain sweetness to life now that I have never experienced, a contentedness that smoothes my way like a gentle wind at my back or a soft light on my face. We are still the same people so the same strengths and weaknesses, ambitions and fears continue to confront us but somehow with vigilance, patience, forgiveness and laughter, we can build something new.

Marriage has become both an ending and a beginning, an ending to the journey of dating and a beginning of all that is to come. Marriage has become a sweet dessert, the perfect, hoped-for, anticipated, relished end to dating but also the promise of tomorrow's starters, of tomorrow's meal and tomorrow's celebratory sweet ending. Indulge in these desserts. Indulge in marriage, its joy and sorrows, its trials and triumphs, its fidelity and longevity. Persevere to sweet endings and prepare sweet tidings for each other. Be happy, make moments to savour and always slice an extra large piece of cake, lay two forks on the plate and share laughter and good food with one another.

When I was a teenager, I worked at a summer resort for seniors in the country, near where I was raised. The place seems like a dimly remembered dream now, a place from the past, a place where I spent every summer during high school, earning money to pay for school clothes and to save for university. Friendly Acres, yes that is what it was actually called, was a sort of summer camp for seniors. It provided an opportunity for seniors who typically lived in the city all year long a chance to escape to the country for twelve days, to enjoy the peace and quiet, to take daily excursions, to eat hearty meals, to get some youthful colour back in their cheeks, to feel less alone. The place was sponsored by a church in the city and their days were filled with song, crafts, prayers, entertainment and the great outdoors.

It was my first paying job and, when I started, I worked as a gardener which, to be honest, I was little more than a weed puller. I spent many lazy, hot, July and August afternoons sitting between rows of green beans or tomatoes, weeding and day dreaming. My third summer, Marilyn, the woman who ran the place, asked me if I wanted to work in the kitchen. I remember so clearly that kitchen with its big, eight burner gas stove, the chipped, white enamel cupboard doors, the clanging noise of the pots in drawer when I had to pull too hard to get it unstuck, and the little wisps of white flour that were always in the corners under the window.

It was in that kitchen that I learned to cook. I perfected my pie pastry recipe while listening to the wisdom of old women who insisted my pastry flaked so well and was so light because I had it "in my hands". Pie pastry became a great mystery and a blessing bestowed on the very lucky who had the right hands. I learned to make stews, bread puddings, and cookies without end. We served three meals a day and a morning and afternoon snack. Tuesdays I would bake bread, Thursday pies for the weekend. Because the guests only came for twelve days, another busload would arrive and the menu would start again. I had a lot of practice!

In the dining room, we had a rope which hung from the ceiling and when pulled would ring a bell atop the peak of the roof, calling the seniors to dinner. The newest guests would wait for the bell before coming to the dining room but the old hands would already be on their way up from the lodge, like cows coming back to the barn at twilight. We sang grace before every meal to remind us all to be thankful for the food we eat. We had a large pass-through from our counters into the dining room so we could watch the diners enjoy their meal and gauge when to serve dessert. Through that window, I would watch the winter-thin become plump, the pale become rosy and the quiet become talkative as the days passed. And when finally they were heading home again, they did so rested, fuller, healthier and re-connected. It was at Friendly Acres that I learned that good food and eating together connects us, creates community, heals unseen ills, animates us and gives us the strength to return to our daily lives.

Pie pastry

Lessons to the uninitiated and ambitious: have your shortening at room temperature, sifting flour really does make a difference, handle it lightly and shortly, never knead, vinegar helps flaking, a chilled pie to a preheated hot oven pops, pie is best shared.

4 ½ cups pastry flour
pinch of salt
1 lb lard (or 1 package Tenderflake)
1 egg beaten
1 tbsp white vinegar
cold water

Sift flour and salt. Add lard and cut into flour. I use my hands but you could certainly use a pastry cutter. Cut in the flour until it has the consistency of baby powder. In a one cup measure, beat the egg with a fork and add the vinegar. Fill the one cup measure with cold water until you have one full cup. Add to the flour and lard mixture. Combine until you have one firm ball. Do not knead the dough, in fact try to minimize how much you handle the dough.

When it is time to roll out the flour use one additional cup of flour to dust the counter or marble slab. The addition of this flour during rolling will be the exact amount of flour you will need to make tender, flaky pastry every time.

Another trick is to roll out and use the pastry and refrigerate the pie or tarts. Take the chilled dish from a cold fridge and put it in a hot preheated oven. This process will help make the pastry flake even more during baking.

Better butter tarts

It has been a Christmas baking miracle around here! You should smell the house right now, delicious. We got on a roll today, a good day to stay home and bake. Outside, cold, small frigid flakes swirling around, in my opinion the kind of day to stay indoors and cook! First thing, a batch of chocolate chip cookies to eat while baking with a large icy cold glass of milk. My guy joined me at the kitchen bar and helped time recipes, shape cookies on sheets and taste test as they came out of the oven. So far, we have made coconut magic bars with butterscotch and chocolate chips, brownies with a chocolate oatmeal crust on the bottom and peanut butter icing, butter cookies with hazelnuts, coconut and cranberries, peanut butter cookies, chocolate cookies with macadamia nuts. Banana bread is waiting to go in the oven and I think we will make some chocolate drops as well tonight, a perennial favourite from my childhood. This week I still want to make some Skor bars, Sweet Marie bars, cherry nut bars, spice cookies and homemade butter tarts. I absolutely love butter tarts; it is always a challenge not to eat them as they come from the oven. For lots of desserts I can make them and then enjoy watching others enjoy them but butter tarts are a real weakness of mine! It has been a great afternoon, especially after two hours of ironing this morning, ugh! Christmas is a great excuse to dust off your favourite dessert recipes and indulge in making them all.

Pie pastry
1 cup raisins
½ cup melted butter
2 eggs
½ cup brown sugar
½ cup light corn syrup
½ tsp vanilla

Roll out the pastry. Using a large juice glass or pastry cutter, cut pastry rounds and mould to shape into muffin tins. Flute and fold edges to ensure fit of pastry in tin.

To begin, put raisins in small bowl and cover in boiling water. When raisins are plump, after approximately 5 minutes, drain and place the raisins evenly in the pastry shells to cover the bottom of the shells. Melt butter and in medium bowl beat butter, eggs, brown sugar, syrup and vanilla. Pour into shells covering the raisins to 2/3 full. Bake in oven at 350F degrees for 15 minutes.

Tea biscuits

Make homemade tea biscuits; do not be afraid of them, just make them. Make mistakes. Perfect them. They are worth the effort. Serve them hot with butter and honey, smother them in homemade jam or add cheese and dill for a change. Roll them thick before cutting and baking. Watch them rise to the heavens. My grandmother and Aunt Irene would compete over whose tea biscuits were better, taller, fluffier. They were a source of pride and fierce contest. Enter the ring; perfect your own. You will thank me.

4 cups flour
4 tsp cream of tartar
2 tsp baking soda
pinch of salt
1 cup butter
¼ cup sugar
2 eggs, beaten
1 ½ cups milk

Sift dry ingredients. Add sugar and stir. Stir in eggs and milk. Mix to a soft dough, do not over mix or knead. Roll out gently, cut into size required with large juice glass or pastry cutter. Bake in a 450 degree oven for about 10 minutes on an un-greased baking sheet. Delicious hot from the oven.

We stopped at a dear friend's, a friend from my university days, for a Christmas tea. It was a great time, the tree twinkling softly in the corner, soft lights, hot teas, plates full of food balanced on your lap and endless laughter and stories. I sat there, thoroughly enjoying myself, and the whole experience reminded me of why I love high teas and the first time I ever experienced one. To be honest, the first time I had a high tea was only two years ago and it has already become a tradition. Two summers ago, while we were dating, my guy and I took a trip to England to meet and visit with his uncle and aunt in Paignton, Devon, down along the south coast of England. It was a perfect English summer, clear blue skies, warm days, no rain, vibrant green fields and the sea, always the sea, beyond the cliffs, shining in the sun. We saw ponies on the moors, sailed down the river Dart, feasted in small bakeries, supped on carvery, sampled pear and apple ciders, gulped down cockles in paper cups sold from chip trucks by the sea all washed down with beers galore. I had chip butties, and eggs and chips, and real Cornish pasties sitting on the breakwater in Padstow in Cornwall.

One brilliant afternoon, I was introduced to the glories of the high English cream tea. We traveled over to Torquay and, at shortly past three, we entered the Grand hotel, a majestic old place with a terrace on which we sat that overlooks the sparkling bay. I remember feeling the breeze from the sea and knowing that this moment would make a memory. Shiny pots of tea arrived, carried by waiters in black and whites, the shirts still starched, the bow ties unloosened. White crockery cups, small plates piled in delicate almond cookies, sugar in cubes. That tea went down fine, somehow appropriate, calling us to slow down. Soon, plates of finger sandwiches arrived, lean, rare beef with horseradish, cheese and pickle, tomato and cream cheese, water crest and cheese, all fanned before us. Honestly, in normal circumstances, I would have eaten the entire plate and looked for more, but just then, it was enough. Just when it seemed complete, carried before them in the place of honour, the waiters placed the cream scones before us, impossibly high, golden brown on all sides, dusted as if blown on the breath of babies with powdered sugar. Tubs of Devon cream nestled beside pots of home made strawberry jams. I make my own strawberry jam every year and can appreciate a good, full fruit jam, the berries still retaining the sun in the fields. I remember cutting the scones, flakes falling from my knife, and then covering them with cream and jam. That first magical taste and I was hooked. Each bite required another slathering of cream and jam and all too soon the scone was gone and I was left only with its memory. Even now, I can recall exactly how it was to sit there, on that terrace, the breeze from the sea, the sun bouncing of the water, the tea warm in my hand, the scone light between my fingers, the cream and jam still on my lips, family beside me, my guy smiling from across the table, the perfect English tea. And now it is a tradition we carry here in our home and in the homes of our friends. Food is magical sometimes and causes us to change; it can shape and twist and reform our life by adding its texture and its meaning to the everyday.

Old fashioned apple pie

My father always baked the pies for holidays, special occasions or Sunday dinners. Ester, Christmas, Thanksgiving would always see my father, a day ahead, in the kitchen, his work-scarred hands sifting flour and mixing pastry or seated at the table a pile of apples in front of him, slowly being peeled and cored. We would fight for the long strips of skin, removed in one long piece with his paring knife, held aloft over our tilted back heads, like red worms being lowered into our open, waiting mouths. All his pies are good; apple is his favourite and perhaps his most perfect creation.

Pastry for one double crust pie
8 tart apples, pared and sliced
1 cup sugar
2 tsp flour
dash nutmeg
½ tsp cinnamon
2 tbsp butter

Preheat oven to 400F degrees.

Roll out and line a 9 inch pie pan. Arrange apples in shell. Mix sugar, flour and spices together and sprinkle evenly over apples. Dab with butter on top. Roll out top of pie, dab edges of lower crust with water to make a seal and place top crust firmly over bottom pressing evenly around edges. Cut a crescent or a leaf in the centre of the pie to allow steam to escape. Cut off excess and flute or crimp edges. Bake for 45 minutes or until apples are tender and bubbly.

Coconut cream pie

Of all the pies baked in my childhood home, this pie is one to bake for my father. Not all that popular any longer, it was a favourite of my father and uncles. It is creamy and redolent with the taste and smell of toasted coconut. Take the chance and prepare this old favourite and enjoy the surprised looks of delight on the face of your guy when he tastes it.

1 baked 9 inch pie shell
2/3 cup sugar
½ cup flour
3 egg yolks, slightly beaten
2 cups milk
1 tsp vanilla
1 cup whipping cream, whipped and sweetened to taste
toasted shredded coconut

Mix sugar and flour in top of a double boiler. Combine egg yolks and milk. Stir into flour mixture and blend well. Cook over hot water until thickened, stirring constantly. Cover and cook 10 minutes longer. Cool slightly and add vanilla. Pour into pie shell and cool in refrigerator. Just before serving, spread whipping cream over filling and top with coconut.

Bourbon pumpkin pie

Add a little southern flair to the classic pumpkin pie. It may never replace your mother's recipe but may easily become a favourite, close second!

2 tbsp butter
¾ cup sugar
3 eggs
¼ tsp ground ginger
¼ nutmeg
½ tsp cinnamon
1 cup canned pumpkin
1 cup evaporated milk or cream
¼ cup bourbon whiskey
1 9 inch unbaked pie shell

Preheat oven to 450F degrees.

Cream butter and sugar. Add eggs, one at a time, beating after each addition. Add remaining ingredients beating well. Pour into pastry shell and bake at 450F degrees for 10 minutes. Reduce heat to 325F degrees and bake for another 45 minutes or until custard is set and firm in the centre.

Rhubarb pie

Taste a piece of rhubarb raw and feel yourself pucker, dip one in sugar and think of me as a child sitting on the stoop, dipping a stalk into the sugar bowl when my mother was not looking, taste this pie and rejoice at how succulent this pie can be. If your pie does not bubble over, you are missing the best part of spring.

Pie pastry
4 cups fresh rhubarb, leaves removed, washed, chopped
1 cup sugar
3 tbsp flour

Preheat oven to 450F degrees.

Line a deep pie plate with pastry. Layer chopped rhubarb in it to form a large mound. Mix together sugar and flour and sprinkle evenly over the rhubarb. Wet edges of bottom crust, cover with a top crust and flute or crimp. Slice an opening in the top of the pie, perhaps in the shape of a leaf, to allow steam to escape. Bake in a hot oven (450F degrees) for first 10 minutes, reduce heat to 350F degrees and bake for 40 minutes longer or until rhubarb is tender. This pie will often bubble over!

I just finished making an upside down rhubarb cake to take to dinner tonight at my brother and sister-in-laws. It smells so good baking right now. I just love rhubarb and as I was making it this morning with chopped frozen homegrown rhubarb that I took out of the freezer, I was thinking about how many associations I have with it. This cake I am baking is one of my favourites, moist, flavourful, with crunchy, sweet topping, great with vanilla ice cream. My mother used to make rhubarb sauce in the spring for us, boiled down rhubarb sweetened with sugar and served in a bowl or over ice cream. I remember pulling it by the stalk from the ground and biting into that sour, stringy stalk and running to the door to plead for a small bowl of sugar to dip it into and sitting on the front stoop dipping and chewing and thinking it was the best treat. But more than all, it is that first rhubarb pie of the spring that makes my mouth water, the tender green and pinkish rhubarb, mixed with sugar, thickening in the pie, and boiling over, dripping and hissing in the oven, the pastry flaking and browning and ending up covered in that delicious sweet sticky, almost toffee textured glaze atop the pie. I love that first bite out of the first pie of the season, the grass still greening, the leaves just unfolding and daffodils in the garden. It is a taste of spring, the last bite of winter, the promise of things to come. The first pie is always the best, no matter how tasty the others that follow are. It is always a taste of a promise fulfilled, that the snow will leave and summer is just on the doorstep. Today's cake is baked in hope of that first pie and the end of this snow. Tonight eating it with family no one else will know what hopes I baked into this cake but I will know and, looking around at loved ones, I will know what I have hoped for all of them.

Autumn apple crisp

Apple crisp is autumn days to me – sun-filled crisp autumn days the smell of wood smoke and rotting, brightly-coloured red, orange and russet leaves, bulky, woolen sweaters and apple picking. Apple crisp is for that time in your relationship when you are contentedly settled with your guy, when routine feels right, when hopping in the car on a Saturday morning and heading to the orchard is believed by you both to be an absolutely perfect day.

2 cups all purpose flour
2 cups rolled oats
1 tsp cinnamon
½ tsp nutmeg
1 ½ cups packed brown sugar
1 ½ cups butter
8-10 medium apples, cored and sliced

Preheat the oven to 350F degrees. Core and peel the apples. In a 9 x 13 inch pan, slice the apples, covering the bottom of the pan and filling the pan about 2 inches thick. In a large bowl, combine flour, oatmeal, cinnamon, nutmeg and brown sugar. Cut in butter into the mixture until crumbly. Sprinkle the crumb mixture over the apples evenly, patting gently to create a loose crust. Bake at 350F degrees for 45 to 50 minutes or until apples are tender. For juicy apples at the bottom, sprinkle the apples with a tbsp of additional sugar before adding the crust.

Bread pudding

I learned to make bread pudding at Friendly Acres and am I glad I did as all these years later bread pudding is one of my guy's favourites. We had an old dented deep aluminum pan, blackened with use, that sat atop the shelf over the gas stove. Leftover cold toast from breakfasts or heels of loaves would be thrown inside throughout the week, growing even staler. Once a week, I would break these castaways into cubes and make a hot, toasted pan of pudding, that old kitchen redolent with the smell of nutmeg. Strange how life is, learning to make pudding those summers would lead me to a man who cannot get his fill of golden bread pudding.

1 cup raisins
1 tbsp fresh orange or lemon zest
1/3 cup Madeira or dark rum
7 cups cubed white bread, lightly toasted
4 eggs
1 cup sugar
1 tsp vanilla
¼ cup butter, cut into small pieces
Nutmeg to taste

Combine the raisins, zest and Madeira or rum in a small bowl. Let soak about 20 minutes. Butter a 9 x 13 inch baking dish. Place the bread cubes in the prepared dish. Whisk together the eggs and sugar in a large mixing bowl. Stir in the milk and vanilla. Sprinkle the raisin mixture evenly over the bread cubes. Pour the egg mixture over the bread and let stand about 15 minutes. Preheat the oven to 375F degrees. Dot the top of the pudding with butter and sprinkle with nutmeg. Bake until golden brown and set in the centre, about 35 to 40 minutes. Serve warm. Drizzle each serving with heavy cream if desired.

Pail of bran muffins

When I was a child, my mother always had a pail of this batter in a large Tupperware bowl in the fridge in the pantry. At a moment's notice or when it came time to bake for our school lunches, my mother could spoon this batter into baking tins and almost immediately the house would be filled with the delicious smell of muffins baking. I have many memories of sitting in the school cafeteria, unwrapping wax paper-covered muffins and biting into my mother's care while my friends ate store bought wagon wheels. How often did I hear pleading from friends to trade!

2 cups natural bran
4 cups all bran
5 cups flour
2 tbsp baking soda
1 tbsp salt
3 cups white sugar
2 cups raisins or chopped dates
2 cups hot water
4 beaten eggs
1 cup canola oil
1 quart buttermilk

Mix dry ingredients. Add dried fruit. Mix liquids and add to dry ingredients. Let stand for 12 hours in fridge before baking. Bake for 20 minutes at 350F degrees.

Keep remaining batter in fridge for up to two months. Simply scoop and bake additional muffins as needed.

Spiced carrot muffins

Everyone has a recipe for carrot muffins. I have many. They are all equally delicious. What makes this one different is the addition of four spices for a remarkably explosive taste and the addition of buttermilk to give the muffins texture and creaminess. A perfect blend, your tongue will work overtime deciding if this is spice cake or creamed carrots.

1 ½ cup flour
1 tsp baking powder
1 tsp baking soda
½ tsp cinnamon
½ tsp salt
¼ tsp each – nutmeg, allspice, ginger
¾ cup brown sugar
1 egg
½ cup buttermilk or sour milk
1/3 cup canola oil
½ tsp vanilla
1 ½ cup grated carrot
½ cup raisins or walnuts

In a large bowl, measure all dry ingredients. In a separate bowl, beat together egg, milk, oil and vanilla. Stir in carrots and raisins or walnuts. Pour into dry ingredients. Stir until just moistened. Bake 20 minutes at 400F degrees.

Carrot and pineapple muffins

Here is another variation on the classic carrot muffin. I adore all things citrus: orange, lemon, lime, coconut and in this case pineapple. In these muffins, the pineapple adds moisture to the muffin and is a nice balance to the carrot. Similar to my carrot cake recipe, these muffins will become a favourite in your repertoire, easy, dependable and popular with the family.

1 ½ cup flour
¾ cup brown sugar
1 tsp baking powder
1 tsp baking soda
1 tsp cinnamon
2/3 cup canola oil
2 eggs
1 cup finely grated carrots
½ cup crushed pineapple
1 tsp vanilla

In a large bowl, combine flour, sugar, baking powder, baking soda and cinnamon. In a separate bowl, mix oil, eggs, carrots, pineapple and vanilla. Add wet ingredients to dry. Mix well. Bake 20 to 25 minutes at 325F degrees.

Blueberry cobbler

Bubbling cobbler is just good. I like to make it with blueberries because they have a nice dark colour, ooze and bubble and escape into every nook and cranny and make a lovely, gooey mess when baked. Served hot with vanilla ice cream, this dessert is guaranteed to please.

5 cups fresh blueberries, washed
3 tbsp all purpose flour
2 tbsp fresh lemon juice
½ tsp cinnamon
2/3 cup granulated sugar
2 tbsp butter at room temperature

Place blueberries in a large bowl and sprinkle with lemon juice. In a small bowl, combine sugar, flour and cinnamon; sprinkle evenly over the blueberries. Spread blueberry mixture in an un-greased square baking dish. Top with butter.

Topping:

1 ½ cups quick cooking oats
½ tsp cinnamon
¾ cups packed brown sugar
½ cup butter at room temperature
½ cup all purpose flour

Preheat oven to 375F degrees.

In a medium bowl, combine oats, brown sugar, flour and cinnamon. Add butter and mix until crumbly. Sprinkle topping evenly over fruit mixture. Bake for 40 minutes or until topping is golden brown and bubbling in the centre.

Creamy rice pudding

Almost above all else, this is my guy's favourite dessert. A fond memory from his childhood and homage to his English background, he will eat the entire baking dish if left unattended. In fact, I have often found him lurking in the kitchen after dinner, fishing leftover rice from the fridge, pouring milk and sugar over it and hustling it into the oven. This recipe is a more sophisticated approach to rice pudding and the results are magnificent. Once prepared, I am hard pressed to say no to him for seconds.

½ cup rice
1 quart milk
½ cup raisins
1/3 cup butter
3 eggs, beaten
1 cup sugar
1 tsp vanilla
cinnamon
dash of nutmeg

Preheat oven to 350F degrees.

Combine rice with 2 cups of milk in the top of a double boiler and cook over hot water until rice is tender. Add raisins and butter. Combine eggs, sugar, vanilla and remaining milk. Stir into hot rice mixture. Pour into a greased 1 ½ quart round baking dish. Sprinkle with cinnamon and nutmeg. Bake in a moderate oven for 30 minutes or until set.

Peach clafouti

As far as I can determine, clafouti is a French take on cobbler. I am probably wrong and someone will be quick to correct me. Regardless of its origin, I love this dessert, fresh, sun ripened peaches plucked from the tree or from one of those rough wooden six quart baskets, smelling of late summer, fuzzy to the touch and still warm from the sun, washed, peeled and transformed into this perfect summer evening dessert with a great dollop of vanilla ice cream.

825 g can peach slices, drained
1/3 cup flour
2 tbsp baking powder
¼ cup sugar
3 eggs, lightly beaten
2 cups milk
1 tsp vanilla

Preheat oven to 350F degrees.

Grease a shallow ovenproof dish, place peaches in dish.

Combine flour, baking powder, sugar in a bowl; gradually stir in eggs, then milk and vanilla. Mix to a smooth batter.

Pour batter into dish over the back of a spoon. Bake in oven for about 50 minutes or until an inserted knife comes out clean. Serve warm with cream or ice cream.

Grilled bananas with honey rum glaze

Here's an idea: one late summer evening, after dinner, steal your guy away from the ball game on television and ask for his help. Tell him to go in the yard and heat the barbeque. Quickly make the glaze and turn on the coffee. Carry it all including the bananas to the back yard. Slice the bananas; ask him to grill. Brush the bananas; feed him glaze from your fingers. Go inside for bowls and ice cream. Serve them outside with coffee. Use leftover glaze in your coffee. Talk with each other and look at the stars. I guarantee the rest of your evening will be just as pleasant.

3 tbsp dark rum
2 tbsp honey
4 bananas, peel on sliced lengthwise
1 tsp cinnamon
1 pint chocolate ice cream

In a bowl, blend rum, honey and cinnamon. Reserve.

Over direct medium heat, grill bananas, cut side down for 3 minutes or until bananas develop visible grill marks.

Turn bananas and brush with honey rum mixture. Continue grilling, with lid down, for 5 minutes or until bananas are cooked through.

Remove and serve immediately with ice cream.

Lemon raspberry dream

This dessert reminds me of my cousin Lori. All the women in my family make it but somehow I think of Lori whenever I make it. She is younger than I am but I know she makes this one for her children and not long ago she stopped for dinner at my parents and presented a pan to my mother. It is remarkable easy to make and absolutely any one who tries it instantly falls in love with it. I can guess that Lori continues to make this dessert because she too has memories of it from our childhoods and sometimes a dish just becomes family.

1 large raspberry vanilla-cake jellyroll
1 package instant lemon pie filling
1 package prepared CoolWhip

Slice jelly roll into ½ inch slices. In a large glass baking dish, lay sliced jellyroll in single layer to complete cover the bottom. In a medium saucepan, prepare lemon pie filling following instructions on the pot, remove from heat and allow to cool slightly. Once the filling has cooled but not set, pour the filling over the jellyroll slices, evenly covering the while layer. Place pan in the fridge and allow to completely set. When ready to serve, cover the top of the pan with an even layer of CoolWhip and serve.

Cherry nut bars

Ah Aunt Kathleen, this was her recipe, one passed on to my mother and now to me. These bars are a tradition at Christmas in our homes and I cannot even imagine a plate of Christmas baking without these bars nestled snugly amid the other treats.

1 cup brown sugar
½ cup butter
½ cup milk
1 cup graham cracker crumbs
1 cup walnuts
1 cup coconut
16 red maraschino cherries, chopped fine
18 whole graham crackers

In an 8 x 8 pan, line the bottom of the pan with 8 whole graham crackers, covering the entire bottom, as though you were tiling a floor. Set aside.

In a saucepan, combine brown sugar, butter and milk, bring to a boil and boil vigorously for 2 minutes. In the saucepan, to this mixture, add the graham cracker crumbs, walnuts, coconut and cherries. Stir to mix. Next, pour this mixture over the graham crackers lining the pan, smoothing to the edges.

With the remaining whole graham crackers, press them evenly over the entire top of the mixture and press down firmly. Place the pan in the fridge to set for two hours.

Ice with vanilla frosting and cut into bite size squares. Sometimes for fun, I add a little of the maraschino juice from the jar to the icing to tint the icing pink.

Chocolate drops

Here's what I decided this morning. I may not have Nigella Lawson's poise, or Rachel Ray's bubbly enthusiasm or even Martha Stewart's endless creativity (or her large posse of creative types on the payroll). I don't have Jamie Oliver's endless enthusiasm to feed the world, though we do share the same name and love of eating. And I certainly don't' have Gordon Ramsay's fiery temperament. But I do make a mean chocolate drop cookie! The fridge last night was full of cookie sheets covered in waxed paper, chocolate drops cooling in rows. I tried a few, and even though I am losing my taste for sweets with all this baking, I had to stop myself from eating a tray while watching television. There should be a leather restraint or a cute little pink pill we could all use to stop ourselves from over-indulging this season but it is almost one of the great joys of this time of year. Sure we will all be moaning about having to go back to the gym and lose some weight in the new year and we will all promise not too do it again. The fitness police will tell us this is a cycle that we have to break, that somehow carrot sticks and hummus snacks on Christmas Eve are somehow just as tasty as rum balls and eggnog. I understand they have to protect their job but frankly they are wrong. I love this cycle. And I don't exercise in the new year because I feel guilty for eating what I liked, that I only get this time of year, with friends and family. I exercise because it is good for me, desserts or not. And I enjoy the sweets, the meals, the wine, the drinks and the chocolates this time of year because they taste good, because they are a tradition, because I get to enjoy them with the people I love. I say go ahead and eat. I would rather live my life exuberantly than die a thin corpse. Exercise for sure, but in moderation, just like enjoying this season's treats in moderation. Well, sometimes to excess when it comes to shortbreads or chocolate drops but the main thing is to enjoy! I may not be a professional chef with a cooking show to support me, guest signings, tours and books but I know how to make a great plate of Christmas goodies. Tonight, more baking and more sticking my finger in the batter to ensure it tastes great!

2 cups white sugar
½ cup milk
½ cup butter or margarine
6 tbsp rich cocoa
1 tsp vanilla
3 cups quick cooking oatmeal
1 cup flaked coconut, firmly packed

In a medium saucepan, melt the butter. Add milk and sugar. Bring to a bubbly boil. Remove from heat. Add cocoa and vanilla. Stir. Add oatmeal and coconut directly to the saucepan and mix well. Drop by teaspoon on waxed paper covered baking sheet. Refrigerate till set. Quick, easy and delicious.

Ginger cookies

Never underestimate the power of homemade cookies, stored in a jar on the counter in the kitchen. They act like a magnet, attracting wayward children, roaming husbands, cherished girlfriends and gossipy neighbours. They are tokens of care, studded with nuts or chunks of chocolate. They smell of home and taste of love. Buy cookies no longer; bake and share them. These ginger cookies are especially good with a cup of hot tea.

2 cups sugar
1 cup margarine
½ dark molasses
2 eggs
3 ½ cup flour
2 tsp baking soda
2 tsp ginger
1 tsp cloves
1 tsp cinnamon

In a large bowl, cream sugar and margarine till fluffy. Add eggs and molasses and beat well. Add dry ingredients, small amounts at a time, mixing well. Form into 1-inch balls, rolling them in the palm of your hand, then roll the balls in sugar. Place them on an ungreased baking sheet about 2 inches apart. Bake in a 350-degree oven, about 15 minutes, until lightly brown on the bottom.

Coconut pineapple squares

For a taste of the tropics, these squares are tops. I first had a version of these squares at a resort in Mexico with my guy. We were away on our first, inaugural holiday together, two newly dating singles, testing the dating waters amid white sand and palm trees. These squares were served at dessert and I fell in love, eating more each time they appeared. At home, after some experimentation, this recipe was born.

1 cup flour
½ cup butter
1 egg
1 tsp baking powder
1 tbsp sugar
I can (9 oz) crushed pineapple, drained

Mix well and pat into a well-greased 8 by 8 inch pan. Cover with chopped or crushed pineapple. Mix together the following and spread over the pineapple.

2 cups coconut
1 tsp butter
1 cup white sugar
1 egg

Bake 20 to 25 minutes at 350F degrees or until brown.

Applesauce cookies

Most nights, when I am walking home from work, I can smell biscuits begin baked at a local factory, located across the ravine from our house. Walking up the sidewalk and over the bridge to our condominium, I am greeted with the smells of vanilla chocolate or occasionally maple cookies being baked, carried on the wind into my neighbourhood. The smell swirl around you and, if I have one regret about moving to our new house, it is that I will no longer be welcomed home with the smell of cookies on the breeze. One such afternoon, I was overcome, quickened my stride and dove into my kitchen. I had leftover applesauce in the fridge and not long after, a batch of these cookies emerged from the oven.

½ cup margarine
1 cup brown sugar
1 beaten egg
2 cups flour
1 ½ tsp baking powder
¼ tsp baking soda
½ tsp cinnamon
¼ tsp cloves
1 cup apple sauce

Cream margarine and sugar then beat in egg. Add the remaining ingredients and mix thoroughly. With a teaspoon drop cookies onto an un-greased baking sheet. Bake for 10 minutes at 400F degrees.

Banana oatmeal cookies

We have all had oatmeal cookies with nuts, with coconut, with raisins, with chocolate chips. Try these cookies with nuts and bananas. They are meltingly soft, moist and keep well in an airtight container.

1 ½ cups flour
1 cup sugar
½ tsp baking soda
¾ tsp cinnamon
¼ tsp nutmeg
¾ cup butter
1 egg, well beaten
1 cup mashed ripe bananas
½ cup chopped nuts
1 ¾ cups rolled oats

Preheat oven to 400F degrees.

Sift together first 6 ingredients in a large mixing bowl. Cut in butter. Add egg, mashed bananas, nuts and rolled oats. Beat until thoroughly mixed. Drop by teaspoonfuls, about 1 ½ inches apart, on an un-greased baking sheet. Bake 12 to 15 minutes or until light brown. Remove immediately from sheet and cool on rack.

Coconut lime cookies

These cookies combine the tang of lime with the sweetness of coconut but when baked offer the most subtle and sublime tastes on your tongue. They can be made ahead and even frozen. If frozen, thaw thoroughly on the counter before baking. These cookies are a light and refreshing treat.

1/3 cu sugar
3 tbsp light brown sugar
½ tsp salt
2 cups sweetened shredded coconut
2 tsp fresh lime zest, grated
¾ butter, room temperature, cubed
2 tsp vanilla
1 large egg yolk
1 ½ cups flour

In a food processor, mix sugars, salt, coconut and lime until no lumps of brown sugar remain, about 30 seconds. Add butter, vanilla and egg yolk. Process until smooth and creamy, about 20 seconds. Scrape sides of bowl. Add flour and pulse until dough forms.

On a lightly floured surface, roll dough into 10 inch log. Wrap tightly with plastic wrap. Refrigerate until firm, at least 2 hours or up to 3 days.

Preheat to 350F degrees. Line 2 baking sheets with parchment. Slice dough into ¼ inch rounds. Place 1 inch apart on sheets. Bake in oven until edges are golden, about 15 minutes. Cool for 10 minutes then transfer to rack to cool completely.

Banana bread

I store overripe, peeled bananas in little plastic sandwich bags in my freezer. My guy thinks our freezer has become some sort of banana wasteland, a desert where old bananas languish, encased in their plastic wrappings, become wedged in corners, slipping down cracks between meat and bags of frozen vegetables, always being tossed aside when you are searching for something else. But when they are rehabilitated and revived from this frozen tomb, they transform into this most enticing, mouth-watering banana bread.

¾ cup white sugar
1 ½ cup ripe banana, mashed
¾ cup canola oil
2 eggs
2 cups flour
1 tsp baking soda
½ tsp baking powder
2 tsp vanilla
¼ walnuts or chocolate chips

In a large bowl, mix white sugar, bananas, oil and eggs until well combined. Add the rest of the ingredients and combine well. Pour the mixture into a greased loaf pan and bake at 325F degrees for 60-70 minutes until a tester comes out clean and the top is cracked.

We spent four wonderful days in Venice following our cruise of the Holy land. Once our ship docked at the port, we disembarked and took a local vaporetto to the land quay at St Mark's square and in the early morning sunlight wove our way through the narrow streets to our hotel. Throwing open our shutters, and leaning out our window, we overlooked endless tiled roofs, the domes of St Mark's basilica gleaming to our left and counted quickly four bell towers nearby. As if on cue, the bells began to toll our arrival and I knew we were in for an incredible time.

To be honest, although we did a bit of sightseeing, we mostly poked along the canals, strolling slowly together, stopping for frequent pastries. Our first was a lovely lemon creamed, sugary confection that we shared, avidly licking the last morsels from our fingers, drinking cappuccino in the quiet, morning streets. I learned that Italians generally only drink cappuccino in the morning, essentially taking their milk for the day, and for the remainder, espresso was on order. We stopped to peer in store windows at shelves lined with nut and fruit chocolates, sweets, marzipans, giant meringues and nut filled pastries, at rows of cheeses, meats and oils, lined like orphans at a convent door, hair brightly slicked down, with pleading eyes, hoping to be chosen and taken home. Bouquets of fiery, red chilies arranged like flowers made me laugh. We ate hot fresh pizzas, seated atop the portable sidewalks stacked around the city, anticipating flooding but just then unneeded, the cheese burning the roof of our mouths as we gulped it down, watching the water traffic near the Rialto bridge. Evenings brought quiet, slow dinners, lit by candlelight, the fruity red wines slipping past my tongue. In grocery stores, I smiled at cartons of eggs; four single eggs nestled together, making me think about our habit of stocking up rather than celebrating food each day with trips to bakeries, cheese shops and butchers.

One warm evening, we settled ourselves at a table for two, outdoors in St Mark's square, the stars shining in the sky, the air warm. Listening to a live quartet of strings play classical and popular music, we ordered refreshments to pass the night. Arriving on a gleaming silver tray, an aromatic coffee for my guy and for me a tall glass of hot chocolate, liquid chocolate to be honest topped with six inches of whipped cream, garnished with shaved chocolate. The carafe of cold water supplied along side was welcome, since this was one rich hot chocolate. I will never forget the feeling of sitting there with the man I love, listening to sweet music, the tastes of chocolate on my tongue, his laughing words; it was a wonderful evening. Food always finds its place at celebrations or in moments of intimacy.

We shared that evening with a woman, a stranger who caught my eye. She arrived in the square, and strode over to a table, her husband, lover or boyfriend in tow, to greet two friends already seated. Her joy in seeing them was evident and I was fascinated to watch her chatting with them, touching their arms to make a point, catching her throat as she laughed, and as if on command, food arrived and added to their pleasure. For ourselves, we spent the rest of our time there, wandering the city slowly, stopping to enjoy food and each other, exploring the local areas away from the tourists, in sunshine and under grey skies, days filled with misty weather. We left in the early hours one morning, St Mark's square flooded, hauling our suitcases upon the elevated sidewalks, the glow of the lamps shining on the dark water lapping in the square. It was a marvelous time, filled with wonderful food, with new sights and experiences, with time spent alone. If you can believe I took as many pictures of food as sights in Venice! It showed me that slowing down is what fills life with its moments, and made me realize that the recipes in my cookbook and the time to create the book both should be filled with a reverence for the moments they create.

Pineapple zucchini bread

The first time I made pineapple zucchini bread, my guy was out for the afternoon and I was alone. I had just been to my little garden plot, aside of our condominium building, and had been greeted with three enormous zucchini that had grew, unnoticed in the shade of their dark green leaves, at the back of the plot, against the fence. Plucking them and plucking up my courage, I had marched into the kitchen and transformed them into this bread, one loaf to enjoy, one loaf to freeze. At first bite, my guy was smitten.

3 eggs
1 cup canola oil
2 cups sugar
2 tsp vanilla
2 cups grated zucchini
8 oz can of crushed pineapple, drained
3 cups flour
2 tsp baking soda
¼ tsp baking powder
2 tsp cinnamon
¾ tsp nutmeg
1 cup raisins
1 cups walnut pieces

In a large bowl, mix together eggs, oil, sugar, vanilla, zucchini and pineapple. Add the remaining ingredients and mix thoroughly. Pour batter into 2 greased loaf pans and bake at 350F degrees for one hour.

Dad's date loaf

Dates remind me of my father. Dad love anything with dates, date squares, chocolate cake with date filling, date loaf. Baking offers me so much. It allows me to show how well I know you. There is more joy in seeing his face light up at a date dessert than in a thousand pairs of socks, however well wrapped. We have forgotten what a sublime gift homemade baking can be.

1 lb dates, chopped
1 ½ tsp baking soda
2 cups boiling water
2 eggs, well beaten
2 cups brown sugar
2 tbsp melted butter
½ tsp salt
¼ cup walnut pieces
3 cups flour
2 tsp baking powder.

In a large bowl, sprinkle chopped dates with baking soda and pour the boiling water over top of the dates. Let soak for 3 minutes. Next add the remaining ingredients and mix thoroughly. Pour batter into 2 greased loaf pans and bake for one hour at 325F degrees.

Herb and onion bread

I would bake this bread every other Saturday all summer long, five years running, in the kitchen at Friendly Acres. Sundays at noon, we would serve Sunday dinner to the seniors, a roast of beef, roasted potatoes, carrots, coleslaw, whatever vegetable was in season, peas and pie for dessert. This wonderful bread always filled the baskets on each table, served hot. Enjoy it with dinner, or, as many of the old timers did, as seconds on the plate, alone, face up, covered with the dregs of gravy and eaten with lip-smacking pleasure.

½ cup milk
1 ½ tbsp sugar
1 tsp salt
1 tbsp butter
1 tbsp yeast
½ cup warm water
2 ¼ cups flour
½ cup finely chopped onion
½ tsp dill weed
1 tsp crushed rosemary

Beat all ingredients together and let rise in a covered bowl for 45 minutes. Stir down and beat again. Put in greased loaf pan and let rise for 20 minutes. Bake for one hour at 350F degrees. Serve warm.

It has been a pretty good day today. I got up early when the house was quiet and my guy still sleeping and padded into the kitchen. I woke with thoughts of fresh bread in my mind. I have always enjoyed making bread and so, this morning, I made some herb and onion bread.

I am fascinated with bread. Sifting the dry ingredients, I watch the texture of the flour change, becoming gradually softer, rounder. Smelling the yeast sponge begin to expand reminds me of change. Mixing it together, I marvel at how the dry and the wet at first clump, grab and finally stick. Rolling it onto the counter in the flour dust is where the magic begins. If you have never made bread from scratch before, you must at least once do so. Life happens in kneading. I know it sounds dramatic but, honestly, there is nothing in this world like the feeling of bread dough under your hands, moving from sticky and suddenly becoming elastic. The dough warms and you can feel it start to breathe. With each knead your body rocks with the thrust and your hands cup this new feeling. You inhale as your rock back and exhale as you push through the dough. It warms further under your hands and becomes something altogether different. You can almost feel the moment when the loaf is born under your hands and you know intuitively that you are finished. I love setting it in a warm bowl to rise, the smell of the yeast diffusing through the kitchen. By the time my guy woke this morning, my bread had been kneaded twice and was ready for the oven. It rose and baked as we sat talking, sipping coffee.

Now that I am married, I think bread is starting to mean something else to me. In making it, I realize that it teaches me, through my hands, that I can add to our life, that I can shape our future, that I can create something entirely new from seemingly unrelated ingredients, create something that will sustain and support us. It is a determined act to bake bread when it is easily and more cheaply found at the grocery store but I believe it is this same determined action to create from scratch something new which will be the same impulse I need to make my marriage grow.

Hot cross buns

There is something intensely satisfying about preparing these buns. Be aware of yourself as you make them. Slow down and take the time. Marvel at the life-giving energy of yeast. Notice the smell of scalded milk. Feel the dough under your hands and the slight ache in your arms. Have patience while the dough rises and reflect on the mystery of Easter. Watch them turn golden in the oven and decorate the crosses with your own hands. These buns are far superior to any at the grocery and will taste all the sweeter.

1 cup milk
1/3 cup butter
½ cup sugar
2 packages active dry yeast
¼ cup warm water
5 cup sifted flour
2 eggs, beaten
1 cup golden raisins
melted shortening or butter
1 cup icing sugar
1 ½ tbsp warm milk
a little vanilla

Scald milk; add butter and sugar. Stir till sugar dissolves and then cool to lukewarm. Sprinkle yeast on water; stir till dissolved. Add to milk mixture. Add half the flour and mix well. Stir in eggs. Add enough flour to make a soft dough and mix well. Knead for 10 minutes. Place in a greased bowl and brush with melted shortening or butter.

Cover and let rise in a warm place till double in bulk, about 2 hours. Punch down. Turn out on a floured board and knead in raisings. Shape into 1 ½ inch balls. Place in greased pans, 1 inch apart. Brush with egg yolk diluted with a little water. Cover and let rise till double in bulk, about 1 hour. Bake in a moderately hot oven, 375F degrees for 30 minutes. Cool thoroughly. Make crosses on buns with icing made from mixing last 3 ingredients together.

Banana doughnuts

These doughnuts are a novelty; bake them for fun. Your children will be thunderstruck that doughnuts can come from their mother's hands and not from a box!

5 cups flour
4 tsp baking powder
1 tsp baking soda
1 tsp nutmeg
¼ cup butter
1 cup sugar
3 eggs, well beaten
¾ cup mashed ripe bananas
½ cup buttermilk
1 ½ tsp vanilla
½ cup flour for rolling

Sift together flour, baking powder, soda and nutmeg. Beat butter until creamy. Add sugar gradually and continue beating until light and fluffy. Add eggs and beat well. Add bananas, milk and vanilla to sugar mixture and blend. Add dry ingredients and mix until smooth. Turn a small amount of dough onto a floured board. Knead very lightly. Roll out ½ inch thick. Cut with a doughnut cutter or cut in strips and press into circles.

Heat salad oil in a large kettle, approximately 4 inches deep. Heat to 375F degrees or until a 1 inch cube of bread browns in 40 seconds. Slip doughnuts into oil with spatula. Fry for 3 minutes or until golden brown, turning frequently. Remove and drain on absorbent paper. Sprinkle with powdered sugar or a mixture of sugar and cinnamon.

Banana cake

Banana cake is midweek dessert. Well banana cake and pie, I suppose. In these days of dieting and health consciousness and food guilt, we have forgotten the pleasure of midweek dessert. A slice of cake, covered in chocolate icing, served with a good cup of coffee, will keep conversation going at the table. Maybe not every night, and exercise, but do have it midweek. The week will not seem as long to the weekend.

2 cups flour
1 tsp baking powder
1 tsp baking soda
1 beaten egg
1 tsp vanilla
½ cup butter
1 ½ cup white sugar
¾ cup sour milk
1 cup mashed ripe banana

Cream butter and sugar. Add beaten egg. Sift three times, flour, baking powder, baking soda. Add to egg mixture alternately with milk and vanilla. Finally add bananas. Bake in a 9 by 13 inch pan for 25 to 30 minutes at 350F degrees.

Gingerbread cake

Nothing smells better baking in the oven than this gingerbread cake, its aroma fills the house and begs you to boil the kettle, make a pot of tea, cut a big slice and sit down to do nothing but enjoy a cuppa and this wonderful cake.

2 cups flour
2 tsp baking powder
¼ tsp baking soda
2 tsp ginger
1 tsp cinnamon
1/3 cup shortening
½ cup white sugar
1 egg well beaten
2/3 cup molasses
¾ cup sour or buttermilk

Sift flour, baking powder, baking soda and spices three times. In a separate bowl, cream shortening and sugar until fluffy. Add egg and molasses. Then add sifted ingredients and alternately with the milk in small amounts until well combined. Bake in a greased 8 inch pan in a moderate oven, 350F degrees, for 50 minutes.

Carrot cake

This cake sounds like a great deal of work but truly it is not. The result is amazing, moist, multi-textured and rich. This cake can be made showy by finessing the icing or every day but either way, it will be the best carrot cake you have ever tried.

2 cups white sugar
1 ½ cups canola oil
3 eggs
2 tsp vanilla
2 ½ cups all purpose flour
2 tsp cinnamon
2 tsp baking soda
2 cups shredded carrots
2 cups flaked coconut
1 8 oz can crushed pineapple, drained
1 cup walnuts or pecans, chopped

Frosting:

6 oz cream cheese, room temp.
¼ cup soft butter
¼ cup milk
2 tsp vanilla
3 cups icing sugar

Preheat oven to 350F degrees. Grease a 9 x 13 or tube pan. Combine sugar, oil, eggs and vanilla in a large bowl and blend using a wooden spoon. Stir in flour, cinnamon and soda; mix well. Fold in carrots, coconut, nuts and pineapple. Pour into prepared pan. Bake about 50 minutes or until cake tester comes out clean. Let cool before frosting.

To make frosting: Combine cheese, butter, milk and vanilla in a medium bowl and blend, using an electric beater. Beat in enough icing sugar to make mixture spreadable.

For a fancier finish, you can cover the iced cake with ground walnut, very flashy.

Apple crisp coffee cake

This is a wonderfully, easy to make cake, perfect to serve friends who drop in or at a family get together. But the best part, the house smells fantastic for hours afterward, the smell of apples and cinnamon pervading every room. Your mouth will water as soon as you step through the door.

Crisp Topping:

1 cup chopped pecans
¾ cup flour
¾ cup brown sugar
½ cup butter, melted
½ tsp cinnamon

Cake:

2 cups self rising flour
1 ½ cups sugar
½ cup butter, melted
1 cup sour cream
3 eggs, beaten
2 tsp vanilla
2 Granny Smith or MacIntosh apples, peeled, cored and diced

Preheat oven to 350F degrees. Grease a 9 x 13 baking pan. Combine all the crips topping ingredients in a mixing bowl with a fork until crumbly. Set aside.

Combine flour and sugar in a large mixing bowl. Stir in butter, sour cream, eggs, and vanilla until smooth. Pour into the greased baking pan. Sprinkle with apples, then crisp topping. Bake 30 to 45 minutes or until toothpick inserted in the centre comes out clean. Serve warm or at room temperature.

Apple and pear Bundt cake with caramel glaze

The Bundt cake seems to have lost favour these days in cooking magazines, on cooking shows and with celebrity chefs. I love the shape of the cake; it provides endless opportunities to decorate at will, tops, sides, filling the centre. It has a regal shape and makes an impressive display. Besides my guy and I both like say the word Bundt and then dissolving into laughter. Any cake that can make you laugh is worth baking.

2 cups sugar
1 ½ cups canola oil
3 eggs
2 tsp vanilla
3 cups all purpose flour
1 tsp baking soda
1 apple, cored and finely chopped
1 pear, cored and finely chopped

Caramel Glaze:

1/2cup butter
½ cup brown sugar, packed
2 tsp milk

In a large bowl, using an electric mixer, beat sugar, oil, eggs and vanilla until creamy. Using a wooden spoon, stir in flour and baking soda until well blended. Stir in apple and pear. Spoon batter into a well greased and floured bundt pan. Bake at 350F degrees for one to one and a quarter hours or until a cake tester comes out clean. Cool on a rack for twenty minutes.

Glaze: In a medium saucepan, combine butter, brown sugar and milk. Bring to a boil over medium-high heat, stirring constantly. Boil for two minutes while stirring. Place cake on serving plate and spoon warm glaze over cake. Serve warm or at room temperature.

Time to take a quick daydream vacation back to a glorious day in Split, Croatia on our honeymoon. I had no expectations of Split, knowing nothing about the city or even the country of Croatia and, wow, what a great surprise. We spent the morning in a small, medieval town about thirty minutes outside of Split named Trogir. How wonderful to wander around the tiny medieval streets, slipping on cobblestones, walking in and out of the bright fall sunshine with my guy. We had a great time and of course took the chance to stop and buy some cherry and cheese pastries. We took them over to a little café beside a marina of sailboats bobbing behind us, ordered coffees and enjoyed nibbling away the morning. I spotted over my guy's shoulder a local grocery store and always one who finds wandering the aisles of foreign grocery stores more enjoyable than any local tour, off I tottered to have a look around. Once I had passed by the café, but before I reached the store on the other side of a busy thoroughfare, I found myself in an outdoor local farmer's market. I was in heaven. I walked up and down the aisles looking at the produce, the fruits, honeys, strings of drying garlic, cheese mongers and deli meats on display. I went back and got my guy and showed him all my great piles of carrots and cabbages that had made me so absurdly excited.

Next we visited an old water powered mill and sampled some local wines, cheese, freshly baked bread and prosciutto. We sat outdoors, by the rushing water, and enjoyed ourselves, throwing the leftovers to the patient geese on the millpond. Finally we found ourselves back in Split where we spent a lovely afternoon wandering the streets, talking with vendors in the fish market, examining the remains of Diocletian's palace and most importantly eating more crème filled desserts on the promenade. The sun was bright on the Adriatic, the wind fresh, and we sat on benches, flakes falling from our mouths to our shirt fronts, amid palm trees, white marble walkways and travelers from around the world. It is so etched in my mind that day, a perfect day for relaxing and desserts.

Chocolate fudge cake

Make this one just for you. Enjoy it guilt free. Decide after the first piece if you want to share it with him!

3 tbsp unsalted butter
3 tbsp dark chocolate, chopped
4 eggs, separated
2 tbsp vanilla
¼ tsp almond essence
2/3 cup castor sugar
2 tbsp rum
½ cup ground almonds
½ cup flour
½ cup cocoa
½ cup castor sugar, extra

Glaze
1/3 cup light corn syrup
1 tbsp unsalted butter
2 tbsp water
4 tbsp dark chocolate, chopped

Preheat oven to 350F degrees.

Grease a deep round cake pan, line with paper. Melt butter and chocolate in a heatproof bowl over hot water, cool to room temperature. Beat eggs yolks, vanilla, almond essence and sugar in a small bowl with electric mixer until pale and thick. Transfer mixture to a large bowl, stir in rum and chocolate mixture, then almonds, flour and cocoa.

Beat egg whites in a small bowl until soft peaks form, gradually add extra sugar, beat until dissolved between each addition, fold into chocolate mixture. Spread into prepared pan and bake for 30 minutes. Stand 5 minutes before turning onto wire rack, leave cake upside down.

Glaze: Combine corn syrup, butter and water in a saucepan, stir over heat until mixture comes to a boil, remove from heat. Stir in chocolate, stir until smooth. Stand until bubbles subside, strain and spoon warm glaze over cold cake. Stand at room temperature until set.

Here we are in old Quebec City celebrating New Year's Eve. It is so wonderful here, in Quebec, I just love it. We have great friends who live here and whenever we have the opportunity, we love to drive up here and have a great visit.

If you have never been here, last night would have romanced you and you would be struck with a French passion. Just after sunset, we all piled in to the car and drove into the old town. You have to picture it here now, the rolling, rough hills covered in mounds of snow, the mighty St Lawrence River slowly flowing to the sea, its surface jagged with floating ice, its waters steely grey, a white smear of freezing mist, rolling a foot above its surface, like a fast swipe of white stark against the grey waters and the rolling dark clouds speeding across the sky. Ahead the looming chateau Frontenac dominates the skyline, the pines across the river, the old city ahead of us. We drove along the river and then descended and suddenly we are in the old city, parking along side the river. We had decided to wander the old cobblestone streets to see the Christmas lights.

The four of us climbed up the long sweeping stairs into the old city. Quebec City remains the only completely walled city in North America and it is truly magical to enter its charms. The old shops, houses and inns, leaning topsy-turvy against each other, sudden little lanes leading off sideways, lit with gas lights, promising adventure, sudden flashes of light as the doors of centuries old churches open and spill people into the snow covered streets, the smells of chocolate and chestnuts in the air, the light snow flakes falling on our scene, it was truly wonderful last night. We ambled along, talking, drinking it in, admiring the white lights nestled in great bows of spruce and pine, tucked against paned windows, resting on great slabs of stone sills. Warm in our coats, scarves and gloves, the city opened up to us and remarkably, you felt like you had stepped back in time, expecting French sailors to appear around the corner, drunk on mulled wine, arms slung around each other's shoulders, or expecting stout French matrons to be rushing their cold children along ahead of them like a child driving fat piglets before them. An hour of wandering left us chilled but warmed with memories, with charm, with grace.

This morning we had galettes for breakfast, triangles of left over pie pastry rolled out and baked and served at breakfast. You toast these flaky morsels and eat them hot smothered in butter and jam or as I like them covered in slowly melting Nutella. We have a day ahead of us of shopping for artisan cheeses, perhaps some Cariboo, a fortified red wine commonly enjoyed here, tourtière, a French pork pie and I always head back home with a car stuffed with pastries, breads and other goodies. It is a food lover's paradise here and for certain the car will have a couple of new bottles of red wine to enjoy once we return. Tonight, we are heading to a traditional French New Year`s Eve party, complete with games, singing, probably the playing of spoons on the knees of somehow who has had way too much to drink, and after the countdown and giving of good wishes for the new year, a groaning buffet meal served to satisfy late night hunger and likely soak up some drink soaked bodies. It is going to be a great time! I love French culture with its dedication to good food, good wine and good company. A perfect place to revel and to ring in a new year filled with thoughts of cooking, food and sharing laughter. I hope you are enjoying wherever you are and wish you a new year filled with prosperity, promise and much love.

www.ingramcontent.com/pod-product-compliance
Lightning Source LLC
LaVergne TN
LVHW011911080426
835508LV00007BA/477